Beginner's Guide to Crystal Reports 2011
A Step-by-Step Procedure

Second Edition

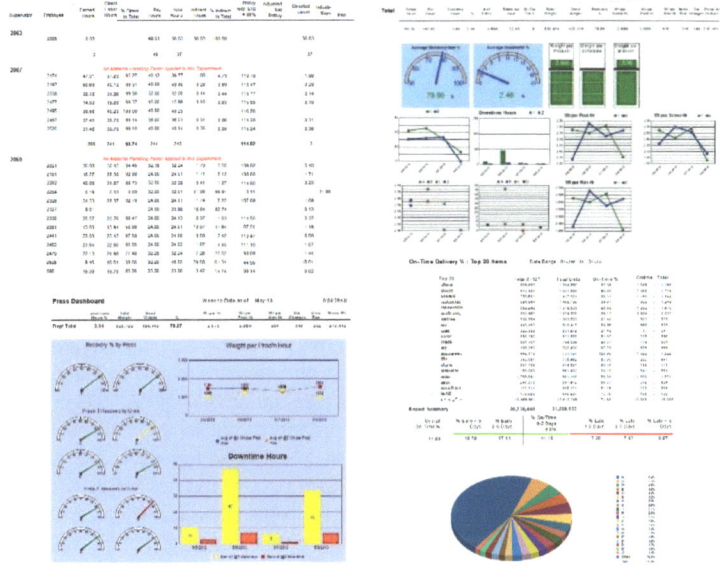

Eric M. Gatmaitan

Ant Illustration: Paul Sizer, Sizer Design + Illustration More info at www.paulsizer.com

© Copyright 2013. SAP AG. All rights reserved. This publication contains references to the products of SAP Business Objects. SAP products and services mentioned herein as well as their respective logos are trademarks or registered trademarks of SAP AG in Germany and other countries. SAP AG is neither the author nor the publisher of this publication and is not responsible for its content. SAP Group shall not be liable for errors or omissions with respect to the materials. The only warranties for SAP Group products and services are those that are set forth in the express warranty statements accompanying such products and services, if any. Nothing herein should be construed as constituting an additional warranty.

© Copyright 2013 Microsoft Corporation. All rights reserved   Used with permission from Microsoft. Beginners Guide to SAP Crystal Reports 2011 is an independent publication and is not affiliated with, nor has it been authorized, sponsored, or otherwise approved by Microsoft Corporation. Windows is a registered trademark of Microsoft Corporation in the United States and other countries.

© Copyright 2013 SaberLogic® All rights reserved. This publication contains references to Logicity® and Logicity Professional®, products and trademarks of SaberLogic®. This is an independent publication and is not affiliated with, nor has it been authorized, sponsored, or otherwise approved by SaberLogic®

This publication contains logo images of Applied IE LLC. Used with permission from Applied IE LLC. The Applied IE logo and swirl are trademarks of Applied IE LLC © 2013 Applied IE LLC Kalamazoo, Michigan. More information at www.AppliedIE.com

About the Author

Eric M. Gatmaitan earned his Master in Business Administration from Western Michigan University with emphasis on Business Information Systems. He also has a Bachelor of Science in Industrial Management Engineering degree from De La Salle University with a minor in Mechanical Engineering.

Mr. Gatmaitan was a faculty member instructing classes in computer technology application, systems analysis & design and programming for the Business Information Systems department in the College of Business at Western Michigan University. In the healthcare manufacturing industry, he served as an Industrial Engineer, Production Supervisor, Plant Manager and Chief Operating Officer.

As a consultant, Mr. Gatmaitan leads projects and conducts training in the areas of Strategic Planning, Business Process Optimization, Quality Systems and Performance Management Systems.

Copyright © 2013 Eric M. Gatmaitan
All rights reserved.
Second Edition
Revision 1.2

ISBN: 1490943048
ISBN-13: 978-1490943046

Beginner's Guide to Crystal Reports 2011

Table of Contents

Introduction 1

Chapter 1: Accessing a New Data Source 3
   Preparing a Server or PC 3
      Tip: View System Type in Windows® 7 operating system 9
      Tip: View System Type in Windows® 8 operating system 10

Chapter 2: Understanding the Data Structure 11
   Data Access 11
   Definition of Terms 13
   Learning and Understanding the Database Structure 14

Chapter 3: Starter Level Skills 17
   Creating a New Report with a New Data Connection 17
   Selecting Tables for a Report 20
   Introduction to Report Sections 22
   Adding Fields to a Report Detail 24

Chapter 4: Basic Formatting of Report 27
   Formatting Data Fields 27
   Adding a Group to a Report 28
   Sorting the Data Records in the Details Section 31
   Adding a Text Object to a Report 33
   Adding a Picture or Graphic Image 35

Table of Contents

Chapter 5: Report Filters and Parameters 37
Filters vs. Parameters 37
Filtering Records to Display 38
Creating Parameter Fields 41
    Setting Up a Report Parameter 43
    TIP: Browse Data 45

Chapter 6: Basic Math Functions 47
Adding Field Data with Running Totals Fields 47
    Creating a Running Total Field 47
    Inserting a Running Total Field 49
Adding Formula Fields 50
    Creating a Formula Filed 50
    Inserting a Formula Field 54

Chapter 7: Summary Reports 55
Creating a Summary Report 55
    Hiding Report Details with Drill Down 55
    Refining the Summary Report 58

Chapter 8: Using Multiple Data Tables 63
Identifying Data Tables Required for a Report 63
Selecting Data Tables 63
Linking Fields 65

Chapter 9: Adding a Chart 67
Creating the Basic Chart 67
Changing Daily Amount to a Monthly Amount 69
Removing the Legend Box 71

   Changing Titles and Labels 72

   Changing the Chart Type 74

Chapter 10: Cross-Tabs 75

   Creating a Cross-Tab 75

   Summarizing Data 77

   Adding Data Columns 79

Chapter 11: Intermediate Skills and Tips 81

   Parameter Field Options 81

   Field Format 84

   Formulas 86

   Running Total Field 90

   Tips 92

Crystal Viewers 95

   Installing and Using Logicity 97

   Logicity® Crystal Viewer Screen Functions 98

Learning Resources 99

   SAP Crystal Reports® 2011 User's Guide 99

   Application Help Utility 100

   Web Community Help 101

Table of Contents

Introduction

Crystal Reports appears as an intimidating report-writing application to managers and even to some IT professionals. This book was developed as a learn-by-doing individual instruction manual. Learning the fundamentals of Crystal Reports can be achieved within a few hours of hands-on activity. The entry-level complexity in learning Crystal Reports is similar to learning Microsoft© Excel. Prior to publication, the contents of this book was used in corporate training to teach non-programmers how to create basic reports.

There are two sets of users for Crystal Reports, they are Report Viewers and Report Developers. Report Viewers are those who access existing Crystal Report files (*.rpt) and execute the file to produce the report. Report Developers, on the other hand, create report templates that define the data connection, columns of data, calculations, summary data and report parameters. Reports with advanced features will require Report Developers to have some knowledge of programming fundamentals.

Crystal Reports 2011 is intended for Report Developers only. Report Viewers will only need a "Crystal Viewer", a free software available at the web for download. Crystal Viewers are software utilities designed to run report with parameter options. Crystal Viewers do not have the capability to alter the design details of the report such as format or formulas.

Introduction

This book is formatted as a work instruction for readers to follow. It is highly recommended to have Crystal Reports 2011 installed and the example Microsoft® Access data Xtreme.mdb downloaded for the reader to follow the step-by-step guide. Use a web browser and type "Microsoft® Access EXTREME.MDB" to locate and download the filename Xtreme.mdb. A trial version of Crystal Reports 2011 is also available from SAP Data Objects.

User proficiency increases each time a new report is developed. It is best to approach the learning process incrementally and explore one feature at a time. There are so many features to learn in Crystal Reports, take time to document each new feature learned using a note taking software such as Microsoft® One Note. Aside from the Help feature built within Crystal Reports, an abundant number of tips and tricks are also available at the web.

This book is intended to provide the reader the basic skills in creating simple reports and the confidence to continue learning advanced skills independently.

Chapter 1: Accessing a New Data Source

Setting up a data connection is the only hurdle at learning and using Crystal Reports. This chapter is intended for Accounting, ERP, or MRP systems using a back-end data source such as SQL. Connecting to Microsoft® Excel and Microsoft® Access data files is much simpler as outlined in Chapter 3.

IT support may be required to perform the initial setup of the data connection such as the ODBC connection. Once a PC or user terminal is setup with the data connection, the report developer can freely create reports without fear of compromising system data.

Preparing a Server or PC

1. Select **My Computer**
2. Select **C:** drive
3. Select **Windows**
4. Select **System32** for 32-bit PC's or **SysWOW64** for 64-bit PC's.

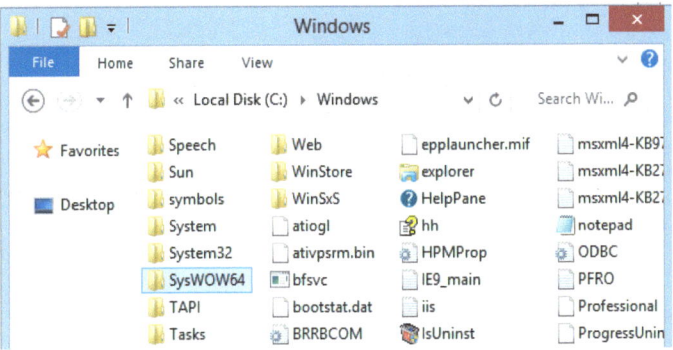

Access a New Data Source

5. Launch **obdcad32** application

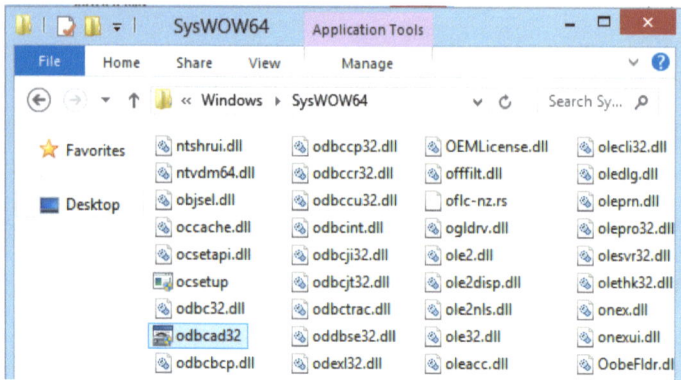

6. Select **User DNS** or **System DNS** tab. Consult with your IT service provider for guidance.
7. Select **Add** to launch the Create New Data Source window
8. Select **Data Source type**
9. Select **Finish**

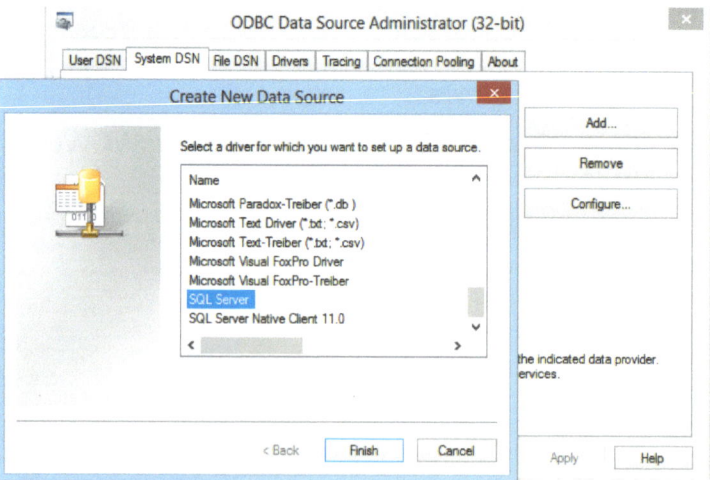

10. Enter **Name** to reference the data connection setup
11. Enter **Description** of database
12. Select or type the **Server Name**. See System Administrator for Server Name.
13. Select **Next**

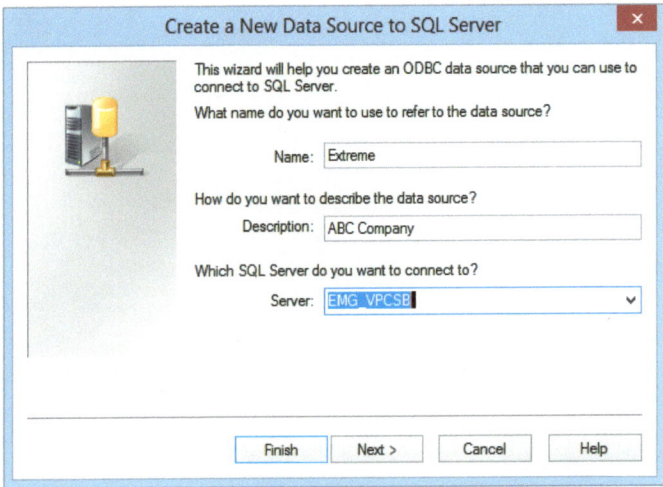

14. Contact your IT Service provider for network permissions
15. Select **Next** to verify data connection setup

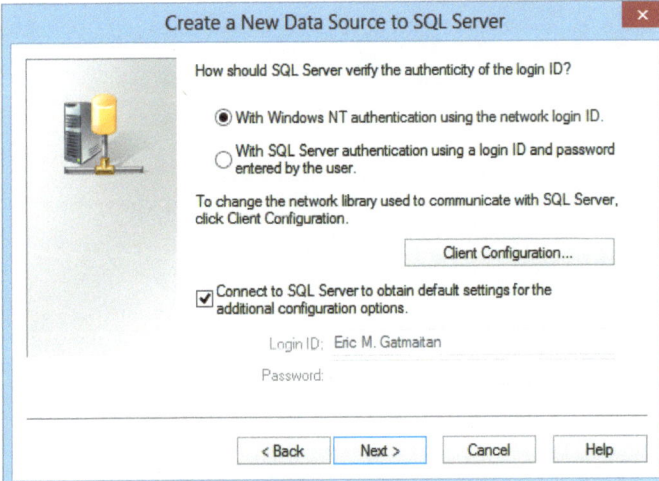

Access a New Data Source

16. Check "Change the default database to"
17. Select **data source** from pull-down menu
18. Select **Next**

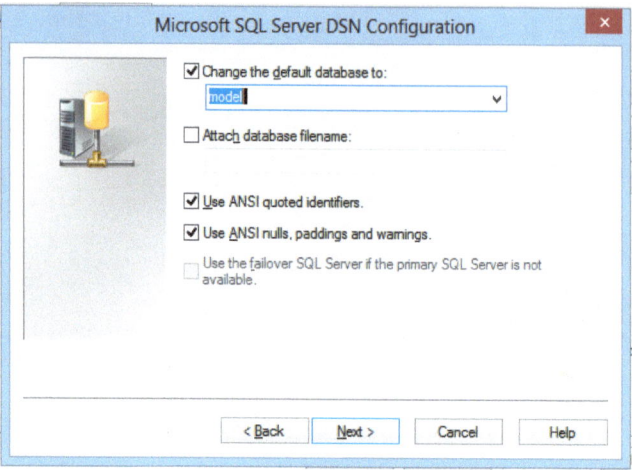

19. Select **Finish**

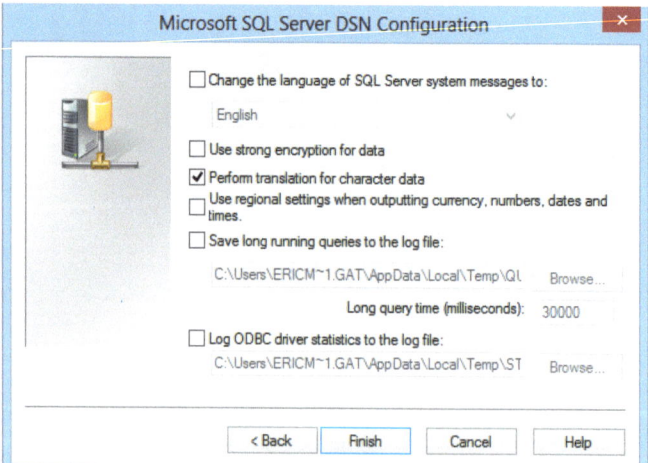

20. Select **Test Data Source** to test the connection

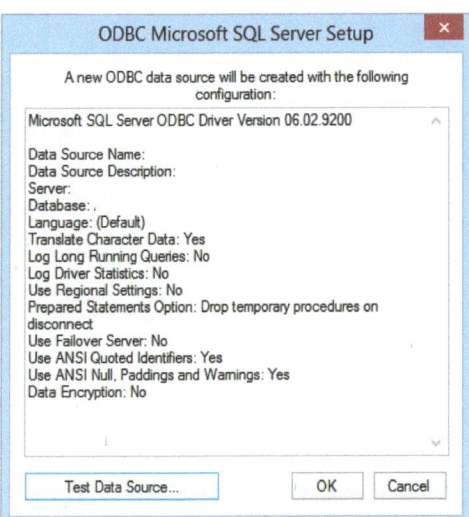

21. Select **OK** to exit SQL Server ODBC Data Source Test. Consult with an IT service provider if test connection fails.

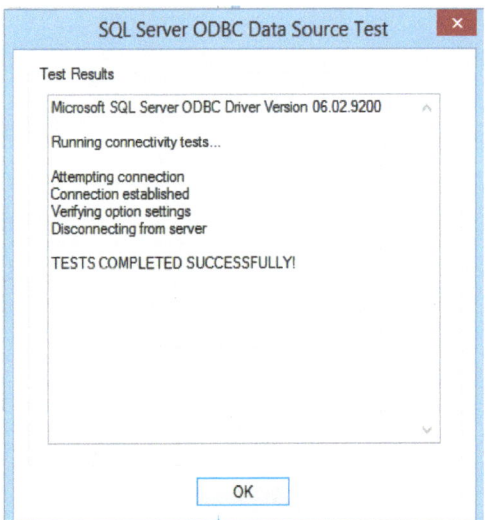

Access a New Data Source

22. Select **OK** to exit data connection setup window
23. Select **OK** to exit

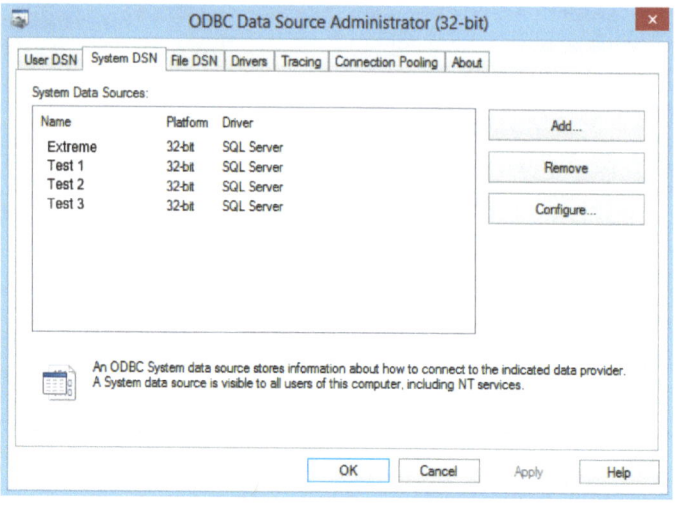

Tip: View System Type in Windows® 7 operating system

1. Select **Start**
2. **Right-Mouse click Computer**
3. Select **Properties**

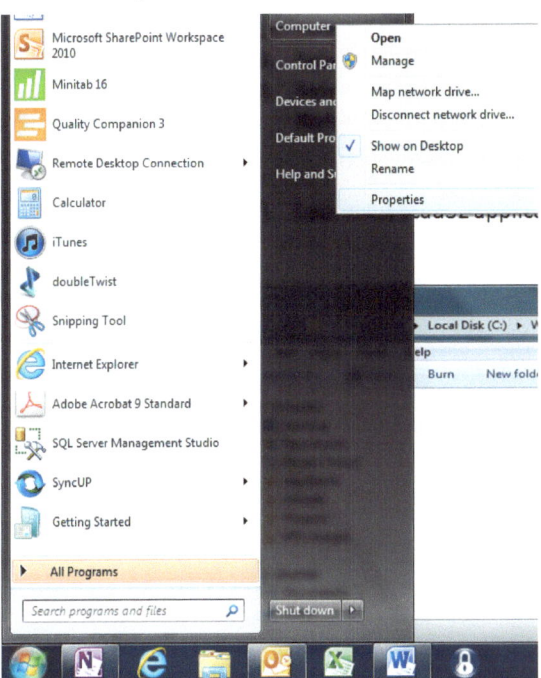

4. Locate **System Type**

Access a New Data Source

Tip: View System Type in Windows® 8 operating system

1. **Point to lower left-hand corner** of the Start or Desktop screen
2. **Right-mouse click**
3. Select **System**

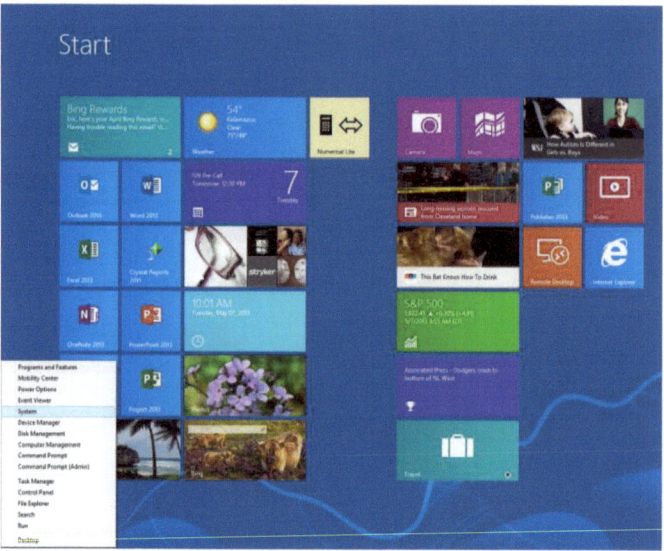

4. Locate **System Type**

Chapter 2: Understanding the Data Structure

Front-end Application and Back-end Database

ERP, MRP and accounting systems are developed in two segments. The front-end application contains the programming codes and the back-end database contains the data tables and view tables. A view table, also known as a query table, is a combination of data fields from multiple data tables.

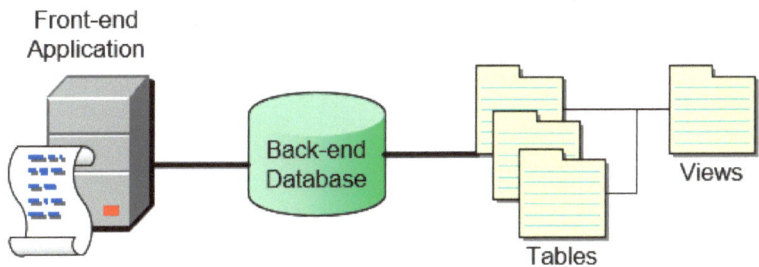

Data Access

Developers of ERP systems and accounting systems embed Crystal Reports as part of the software. Most often, system software will have a utility to add custom reports to be launched from within the application.

Understanding the Data Structure

Having the option to access multiple data sources enables a report developer to merge data from an ERP system, production system, accounting system and even a spreadsheet. This feature opens up a lot of options for data collection and reporting.

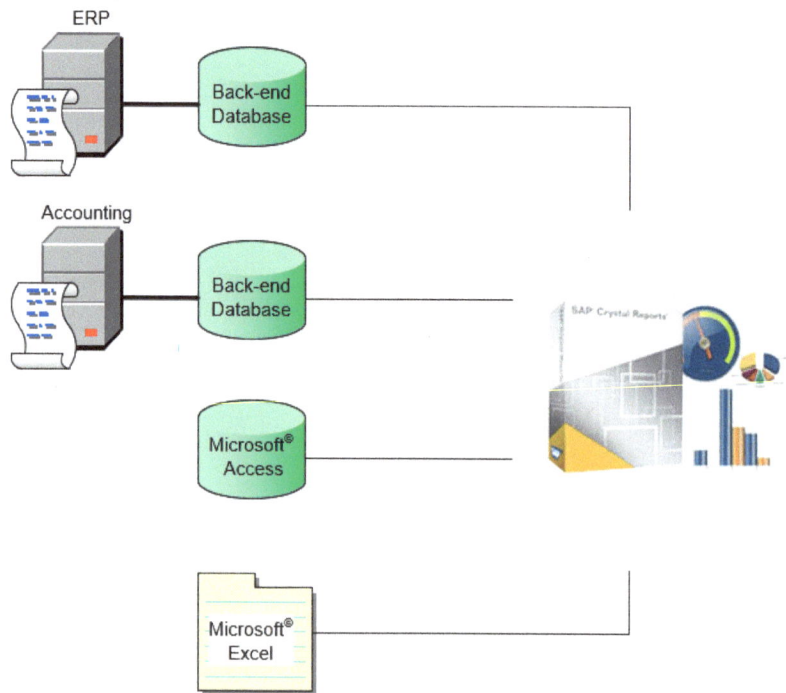

Definition of Terms

Field: Single data element.

Record: Collection of data fields.

Table: A collection of records.

View: A compilation of multiple data tables.

Database: A collection of data tables and views.

Key field: Select field(s) that bind data tables in a database and is used to index a database for fast data retrieval.

Database Index: A data structure that improves the search and access of records.

Direct Access: The process of obtaining data directly with the aid of indexed fields. This data collection process is quicker than sequential access where it evaluates each data record and determines if the data is required.

Note: A Microsoft® Access database file named Xtreme.mdb is used as a data source in this book. The sample database file is available via the web by typing "Xtreme.mdb sample database" on a search browser.

Learning and Understanding the Database Structure

1. Get a list of data tables and views. If not available, contact the software developer or request the IT Service Provider to extract the database structure. Shown below is a portion of the Table Structure of Xtreme.mdb listing the table (i.e. Accounts) and the data fields (i.e. Account Number).

Table Structure for Xtreme.mdb

Account

Name	Type	Size
Account Number	Short Text	8
Account Heading Number	Short Text	8
Account Type ID	Integer	2
Account Class ID	Integer	2
Account Name	Short Text	50
Description	Short Text	100
Account Balance	Currency	8

Account Class

Name	Type	Size
Account Class ID	Integer	2
Account Class	Short Text	50

Account Heading

Name	Type	Size
Account Heading Number	Short Text	8
Account Heading Name	Short Text	50

Account Type

Name	Type	Size
Account Type ID	Integer	2
Account Type	Short Text	20

Bill

Name	Type	Size
Bill #	Long Integer	4
Vendor Name	Short Text	50
Statement Date	Date With Time	8
Paid Date	Date With Time	8
Gross Amount	Currency	8
Paid	Yes/No	1
Tax	Currency	8

2. Review the data table and view names.

    a. Examine the data fields on each table and view.

    b. Examine the data type and comments.

    c. Note the key fields on each data table. Key fields on each table are important when creating reports using multiple tables. The key fields bind multiple data tables to quickly generate the report. Non-key fields can also be used to bind tables and will result in slower report generation.

3. Identify data table(s) needed for a report.

    a. Identify the least number of data tables and/or views.

    b. View tables, being processed query files, may contain the data you need in a single file.

Understanding the Data Structure

Chapter 3: Starter Level Skills

Creating a New Report with a New Data Connection

1. **Launch** SAP Crystal Reports 2011
2. Select **File**
3. Select **New**
4. Select **Standard Report**

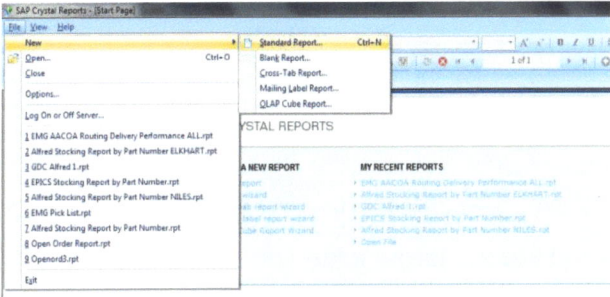

5. Select "**+**" Create New Connection

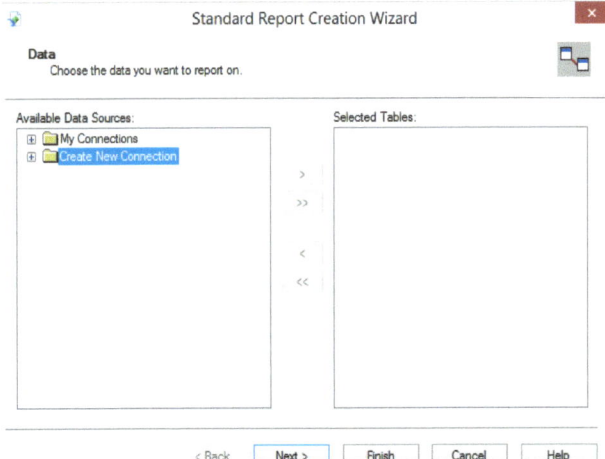

Starter Level Skills

6. Select "+" **Access/Excel (DAO)** to expand options

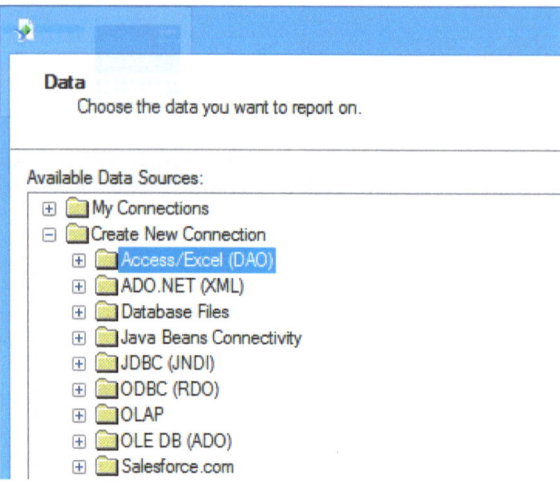

7. Select **Database Name** by clicking on the icon
8. **Navigate** to the target folder
9. Select the filename "**Xtreme**" or the target database name to access
10. Select **Open**

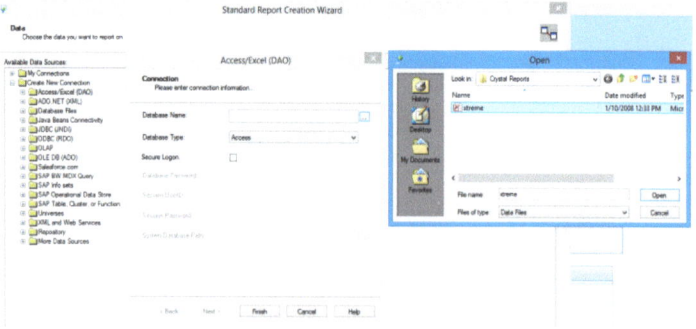

18

Beginner's Guide to Crystal Reports 2011

11. Make sure the Database type is **Access**

12. Select **Finish**

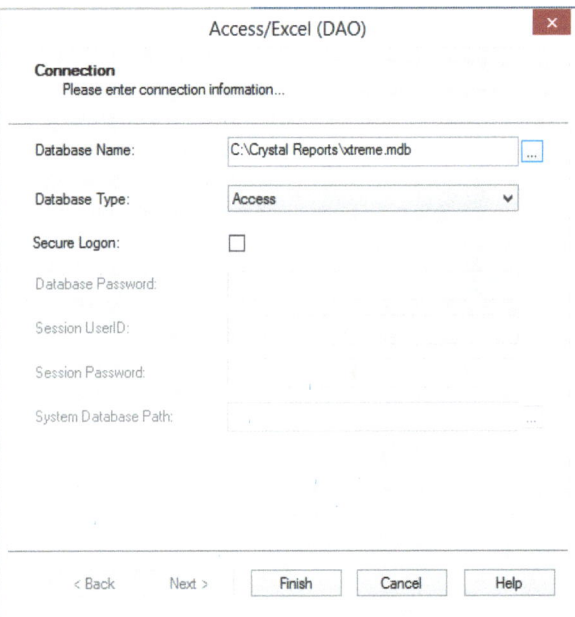

Starter Level Skills

Selecting Tables for a Report

1. Expand the Data Source **Xtreme.mdb** by selecting the "+" sign next to the file path location

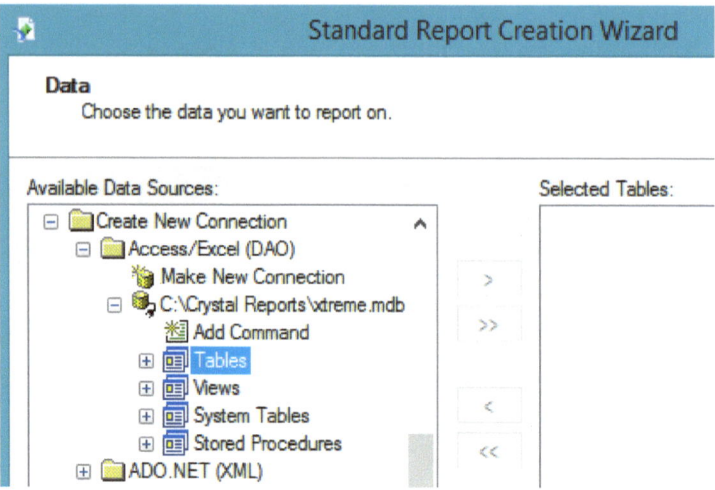

2. **Expand** the table folder by selecting the "+" sign next to Tables

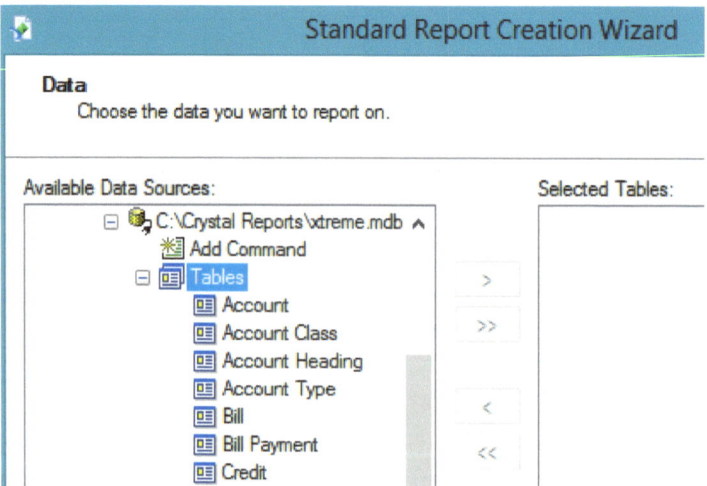

3. Select the table **Orders**

4. Click on the "**>**" to copy the selected table name

5. Select **Finish** when done

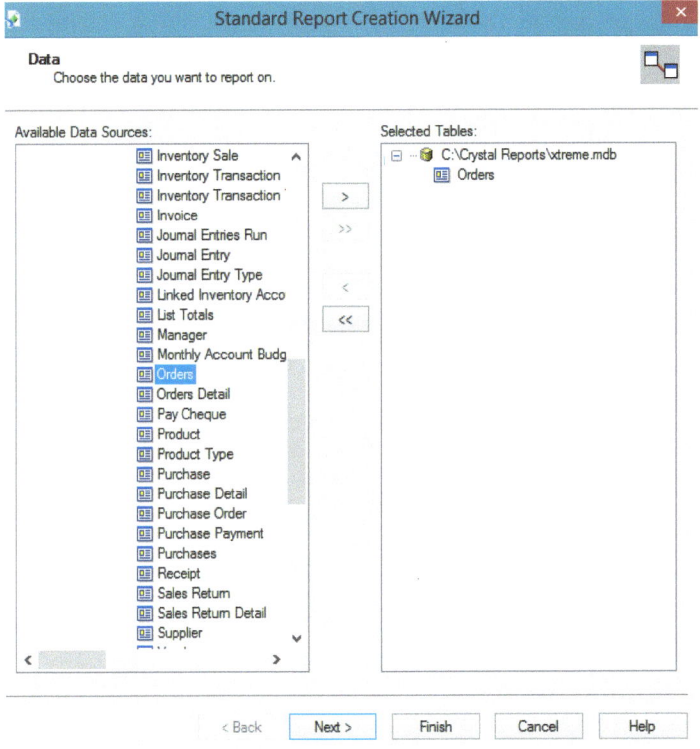

Introduction to Report Sections

In this chapter, the reader will start creating simple reports listing data records in a column and progress at creating summary reports as described in Chapter 7.

Definition of Terms

Report Header : Data, text or graphic items placed in this section will only appear once at Page 1. This section is best used for large reports where basic report information is located, such as the company logo, report title or date range. The succeeding pages of the report are allocated mostly for column data and charts.

Report Footer: Items placed in this section will appear only once at the last page of the report. This section contains report summary data such as report totals or charts.

Page Header: Items placed in this section will appear at the top of each page of the report. It is best used for column headers or field titles. When creating a summary report, the report headers are placed in this section. Items in this section will not show on "drill-down" data sections.

Page Footer: Items placed in this appear at the bottom of each page. It can contain items such as page number, filename, print date or print time.

Details: This section displays the data records and formulas. Format of each field can be varied and placement of data fields for a single record is not limited to a single row. For summary reports, this section is set to "Hide (Drill-Down OK)" as an option for a report user to examine data records in detail.

Group Header: This section by default, contains the group name field. It is displayed or printed on top of each set of data. For summary reports, this section is best used to contain the "drill-down" data headers or field titles. When this section is properly set to "Hide (Drill-Down OK)", this section displays when a report user drills down on a summary line item to view the Details section.

Group Footer: This section usually contains group summary items such as totals or averages. It is located below the Details section. For summary reports, the Group Name field is moved to this section.

Starter Level Skills

Adding Fields to a Report Detail

1. Open Field Explorer by
   a. Select **View**
   b. Select **Field Explorer** or Click on **Field Explorer icon**

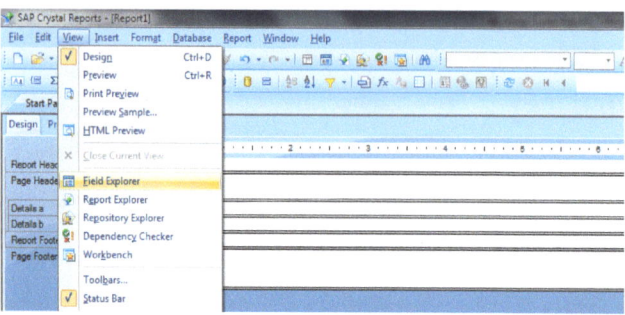

2. Click on the "**+**" to expand the **Database Field** and view the available tables

3. Click on the "**+**" next to the **Orders** table and view the available fields

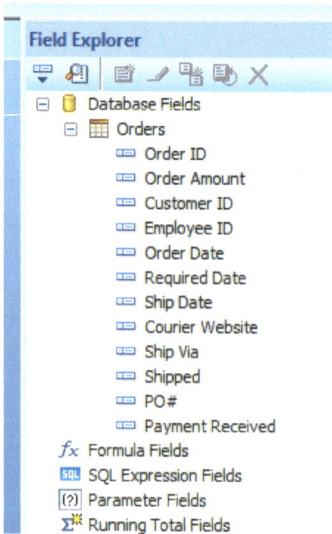

4. Drag the fields *Order ID, Order Amount, Customer ID, Order Date* and *Ship Date* to the Details section

    Note: Text field names will automatically be placed on the Page Header section

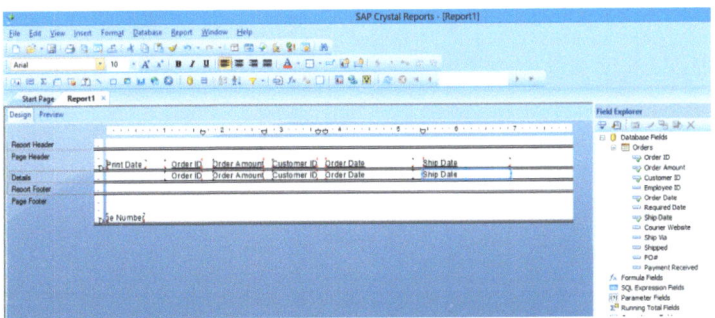

5. Click on **Preview** to view live data

    Note: Crystal Reports is a report utility that has READ-ONLY authority

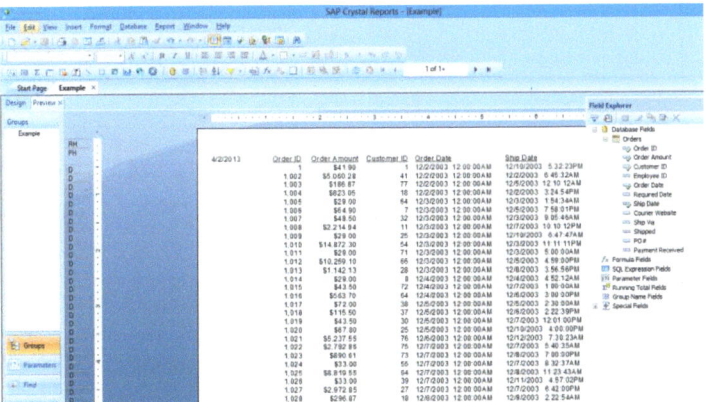

Starter Level Skills

Beginner's Guide to Crystal Reports 2011

Chapter 4: Basic Formatting of Report

Formatting Data Fields

1. Right-mouse click on the data field to format
2. Select **Format Field**

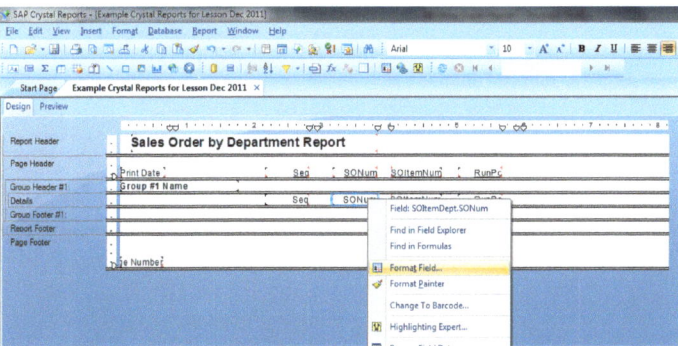

3. Select the format **Style**
4. Select **OK** when done

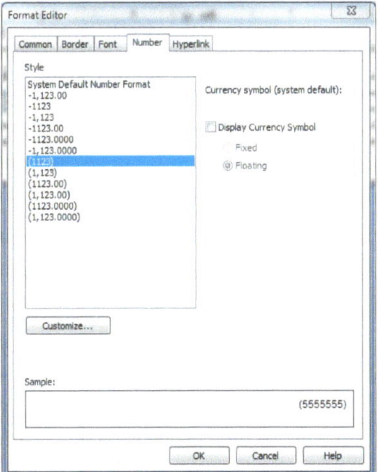

Basic Formatting of Reports

Adding a Group to a Report

1. Click on **Report**
2. Select **Group Expert**

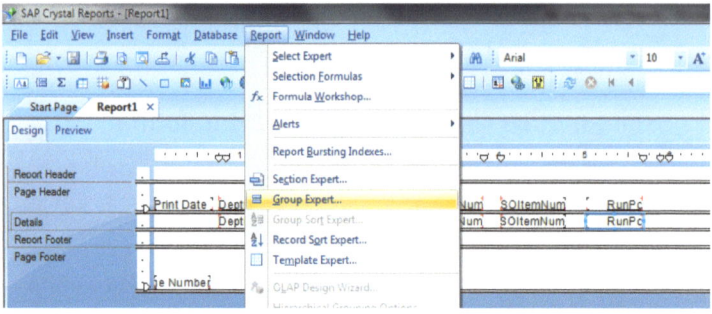

3. Select the field name ***Orders.Cutomer ID*** to Group
4. Click on "**>**" to copy field name
5. Select **OK** when done

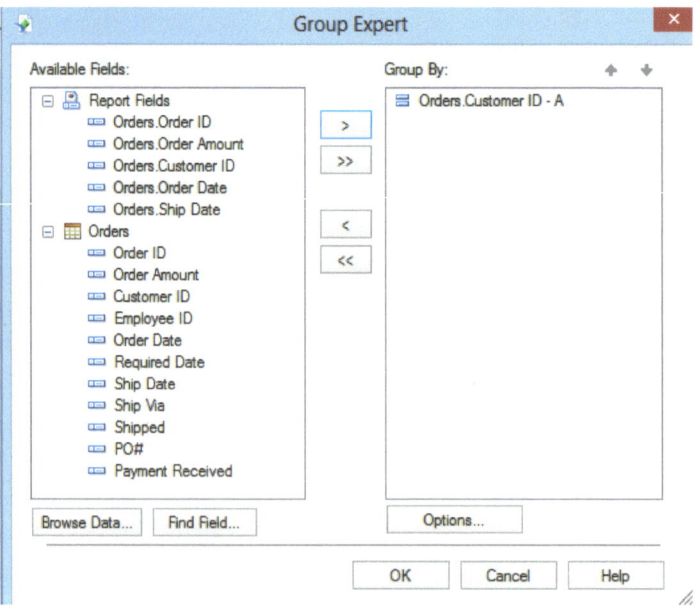

6. Notice the Group #1 Name in the Design view

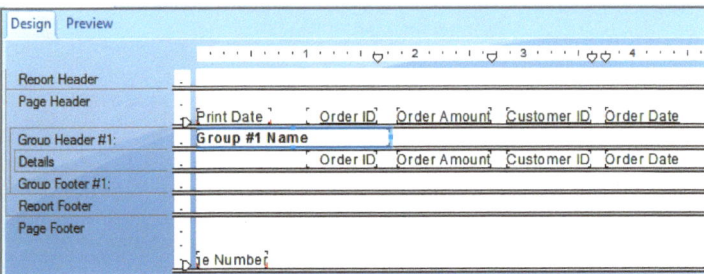

7. Select **Preview** to view report

8. Notice the new report format with Group

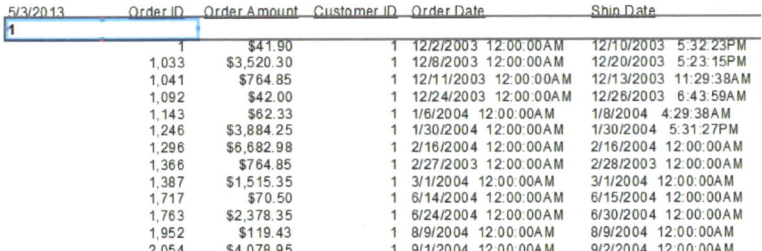

9. Clean-up Details section, if necessary

10. Select **Design**

11. Clean-up Details section, if necessary. To remove a field, select the field and press the **Delete** key

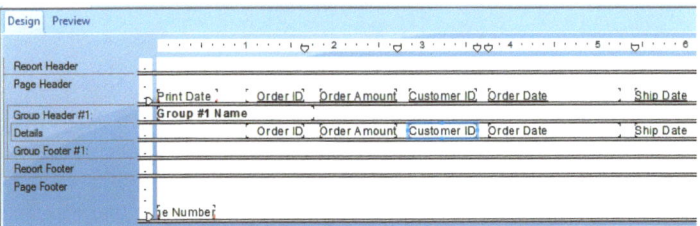

12. Select **Preview** to view report

5/3/2013	Order ID	Order Amount	Order Date	Ship Date
1				
	1	$41.90	12/2/2003 12:00:00AM	12/10/2003 5:32:23PM
	1,033	$3,520.30	12/8/2003 12:00:00AM	12/20/2003 5:23:15PM
	1,041	$764.85	12/11/2003 12:00:00AM	12/13/2003 11:29:38AM
	1,092	$42.00	12/24/2003 12:00:00AM	12/26/2003 6:43:59AM
	1,143	$62.33	1/6/2004 12:00:00AM	1/8/2004 4:29:38AM
	1,246	$3,884.25	1/30/2004 12:00:00AM	1/30/2004 5:31:27PM
	1,296	$6,682.98	2/16/2004 12:00:00AM	2/16/2004 12:00:00AM
	1,366	$764.85	2/27/2003 12:00:00AM	2/28/2003 12:00:00AM
	1,387	$1,515.35	3/1/2004 12:00:00AM	3/1/2004 12:00:00AM
	1,717	$70.50	6/14/2004 12:00:00AM	6/15/2004 12:00:00AM
	1,763	$2,378.35	6/24/2004 12:00:00AM	6/30/2004 12:00:00AM
	1,952	$119.43	8/9/2004 12:00:00AM	8/9/2004 12:00:00AM
	2,054	$4,078.95	9/1/2004 12:00:00AM	9/2/2004 12:00:00AM
	2,142	$46.50	9/25/2004 12:00:00AM	10/6/2004 12:00:00AM
	2,167	$75.80	9/30/2004 12:00:00AM	9/30/2004 12:00:00AM
	2,277	$122.65	10/27/2004 12:00:00AM	10/31/2004 12:00:00AM
	2,337	$68.00	11/7/2004 12:00:00AM	11/13/2004 12:00:00AM
	2,402	$185.20	11/22/2004 12:00:00AM	11/23/2004 12:00:00AM
	2,528	$136.47	12/24/2004 12:00:00AM	12/24/2004 12:00:00AM
	2,640	$2,939.85	1/26/2005 12:00:00AM	1/26/2005 12:00:00AM
	2,659	$659.70	1/30/2005 12:00:00AM	2/1/2005 12:00:00AM
	2,682	$931.05	2/2/2005 12:00:00AM	2/4/2005 12:00:00AM
	2,687	$27.00	2/4/2005 12:00:00AM	2/10/2005 12:00:00AM
	2,772	$2,294.55	2/28/2005 12:00:00AM	3/5/2005 12:00:00AM
	2,900	$5,549.40	4/9/2005 12:00:00AM	4/16/2005 12:00:00AM
	2,982	$63.90	4/29/2005 12:00:00AM	5/2/2005 12:00:00AM
2				
	1,145	$27.00	1/6/2004 12:00:00AM	1/17/2004 6:33:11PM
	1,171	$479.85	1/14/2004 12:00:00AM	1/14/2004 2:39:50AM
	1,233	$139.48	1/27/2004 12:00:00AM	1/29/2004 1:12:05PM
	1,254	$2,497.05	2/3/2004 12:00:00AM	2/4/2004 3:51:39PM
	1,256	$70.50	2/4/2004 12:00:00AM	2/4/2004 9:27:33AM
	1,288	$8,819.55	2/12/2004 12:00:00AM	2/12/2004 12:00:00AM

Sorting the Data Records in the Details Section

1. Select **Report**
2. Select **Record Sort Expert**

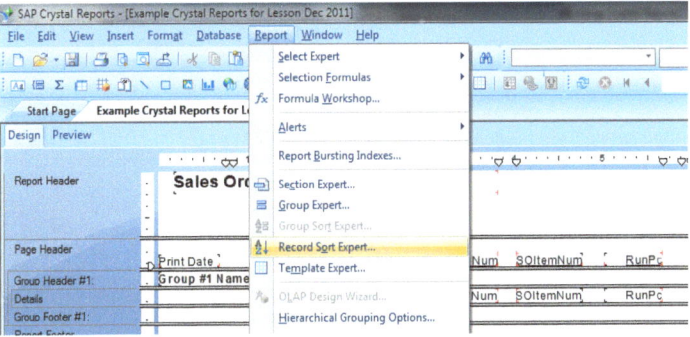

3. Select the field ***Orders.Order Date*** to sort
4. Select "**>**" to copy the field name to the Sort Fields
5. Select **Ascending** or **Descending**
6. Select **OK** when done

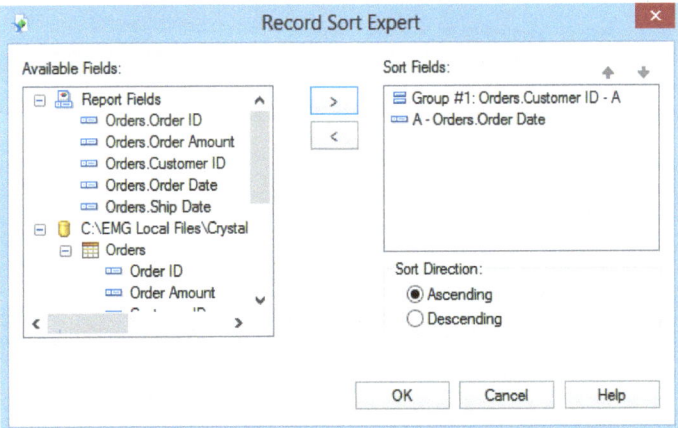

Basic Formatting of Reports

7. Select **Preview** to view the report

5/3/2013	Order ID	Order Amount	Order Date	Ship Date
1				
	1,366	$764.85	2/27/2003 12:00:00AM	2/28/2003 12:00:00AM
	1	$41.90	12/2/2003 12:00:00AM	12/10/2003 5:32:23PM
	1,033	$3,520.30	12/8/2003 12:00:00AM	12/20/2003 5:23:15PM
	1,041	$764.85	12/11/2003 12:00:00AM	12/13/2003 11:29:38AM
	1,092	$42.00	12/24/2003 12:00:00AM	12/26/2003 6:43:59AM
	1,143	$62.33	1/6/2004 12:00:00AM	1/8/2004 4:29:38AM
	1,246	$3,884.25	1/30/2004 12:00:00AM	1/30/2004 5:31:27PM
	1,296	$6,682.98	2/16/2004 12:00:00AM	2/16/2004 12:00:00AM
	1,387	$1,515.35	3/1/2004 12:00:00AM	3/1/2004 12:00:00AM
	1,717	$70.50	6/14/2004 12:00:00AM	6/15/2004 12:00:00AM
	1,763	$2,378.35	6/24/2004 12:00:00AM	6/30/2004 12:00:00AM
	1,952	$119.43	8/9/2004 12:00:00AM	8/9/2004 12:00:00AM
	2,054	$4,078.95	9/1/2004 12:00:00AM	9/2/2004 12:00:00AM
	2,142	$46.50	9/25/2004 12:00:00AM	10/6/2004 12:00:00AM
	2,167	$75.80	9/30/2004 12:00:00AM	9/30/2004 12:00:00AM
	2,277	$122.65	10/27/2004 12:00:00AM	10/31/2004 12:00:00AM
	2,337	$68.00	11/7/2004 12:00:00AM	11/13/2004 12:00:00AM
	2,402	$185.20	11/22/2004 12:00:00AM	11/23/2004 12:00:00AM
	2,528	$136.47	12/24/2004 12:00:00AM	12/24/2004 12:00:00AM
	2,640	$2,939.85	1/26/2005 12:00:00AM	1/26/2005 12:00:00AM
	2,659	$659.70	1/30/2005 12:00:00AM	2/1/2005 12:00:00AM
	2,682	$931.05	2/2/2005 12:00:00AM	2/4/2005 12:00:00AM
	2,687	$27.00	2/4/2005 12:00:00AM	2/10/2005 12:00:00AM
	2,772	$2,294.55	2/28/2005 12:00:00AM	3/5/2005 12:00:00AM
	2,900	$5,549.40	4/9/2005 12:00:00AM	4/16/2005 12:00:00AM
	2,982	$63.90	4/29/2005 12:00:00AM	5/2/2005 12:00:00AM
2				
	1,303	$1,505.10	2/18/2003 12:00:00AM	3/2/2003 12:00:00AM
	1,145	$27.00	1/6/2004 12:00:00AM	1/17/2004 6:33:11PM
	1,171	$479.85	1/14/2004 12:00:00AM	1/14/2004 2:39:50AM
	1,233	$139.48	1/27/2004 12:00:00AM	1/29/2004 1:12:05PM
	1,254	$2,497.05	2/3/2004 12:00:00AM	2/4/2004 3:51:39PM
	1,256	$70.50	2/4/2004 12:00:00AM	2/4/2004 9:27:33AM

Adding a Text Object to a Report

1. Select **Insert**

2. Select **Text Object**

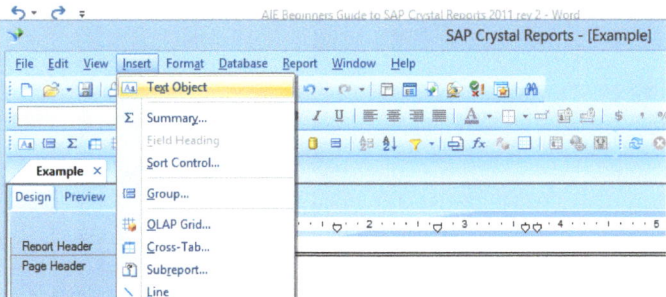

3. Draw the Text Object box on any section

4. Type the text

5. Resize the Text Object box if necessary

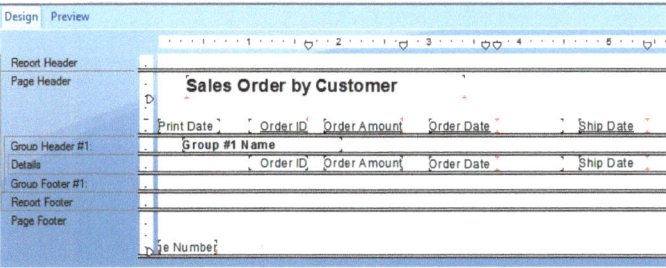

6. Select **Preview** to view the report

7. Reposition or change the font, size or color if needed

Sales Order by Customer

5/3/2013	Order ID	Order Amount	Order Date	Ship Date
1				
	1,366	$764.85	2/27/2003 12:00:00AM	2/28/2003 12:00:00AM
	1	$41.90	12/2/2003 12:00:00AM	12/10/2003 5:32:23PM
	1,033	$3,520.30	12/8/2003 12:00:00AM	12/20/2003 5:23:15PM
	1,041	$764.85	12/11/2003 12:00:00AM	12/13/2003 11:29:38AM
	1,092	$42.00	12/24/2003 12:00:00AM	12/26/2003 6:43:59AM
	1,143	$62.33	1/6/2004 12:00:00AM	1/8/2004 4:29:38AM
	1,246	$3,884.25	1/30/2004 12:00:00AM	1/30/2004 5:31:27PM
	1,296	$6,682.98	2/16/2004 12:00:00AM	2/16/2004 12:00:00AM
	1,387	$1,515.35	3/1/2004 12:00:00AM	3/1/2004 12:00:00AM
	1,717	$70.50	6/14/2004 12:00:00AM	6/15/2004 12:00:00AM

Adding a Picture or Graphic Image

1. Go to the **Design** tab
2. Resize the target area to insert the graphic file
   a. Move the cursor to the bottom line of the section to insert the graphic file
   b. Hold down the left-mouse click when the cursor changes
   c. Expand the area by moving the mouse down
3. Select **Insert**
4. Select **Picture**

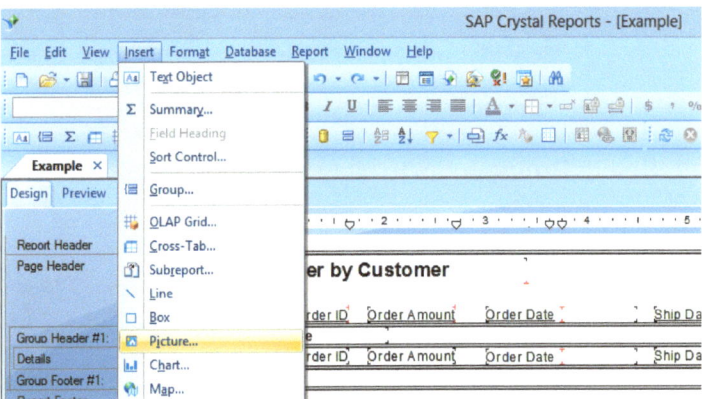

5. Select the graphic filename
6. Select **Open**

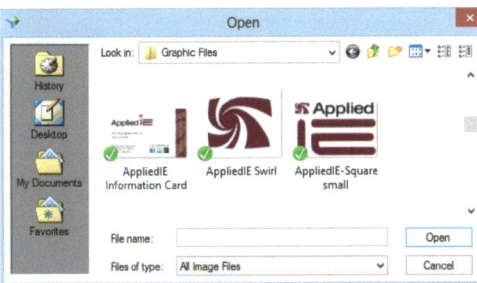

Basic Formatting of Reports

7. Select the target placement area by moving the square guide

8. Click to place the graphic file on the target area

9. Resize the graphic file

10. Resize the section

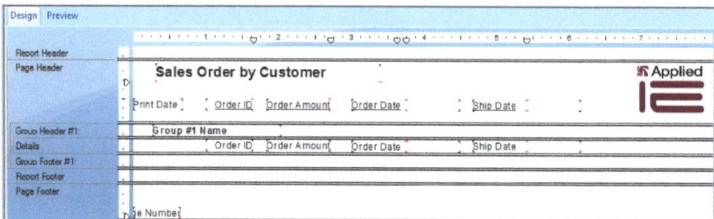

11. Select **Preview** tab to view the report

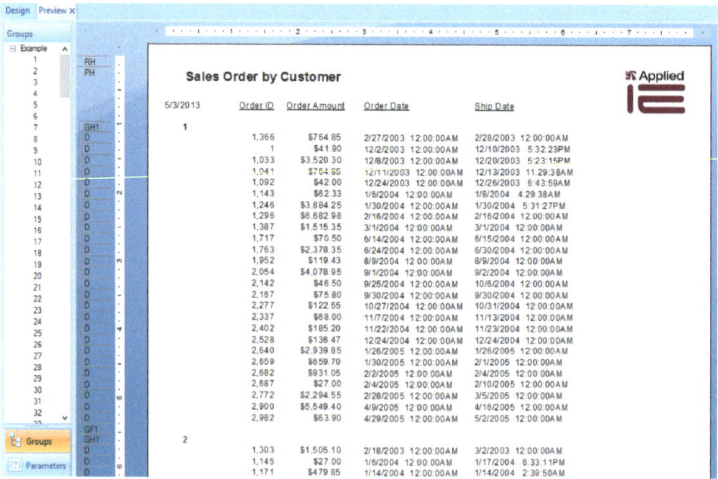

Chapter 5: Report Filters and Parameters

Data selection to show on reports can be controlled by using report filters and/or report parameters. Report developers will initially create a general report using report filters and include a report option for users to enter report parameters such as date range or customer name.

Filters vs. Parameters

Report Filter via Select Expert

Filters select records based on a set of rules established by a report developer. The set of rules identify data fields that meet certain criteria or condition such as <Fieldname> = "Yes". Filter conditions are "fixed" or embedded as part of the report and cannot be changed by report users.

Report Parameter

Parameters are "user-defined" conditions that can be changed each time the report is executed. The report developer creates "parameter fields" to enable users to control the type of data to show on the report. A report date range prompting a user each time a report is executed is an example of a report parameter.

Report Filters and Parameters

Filtering Records to Display

1. Select **Report**
2. Click on **Select Expert**
3. Select **Record**

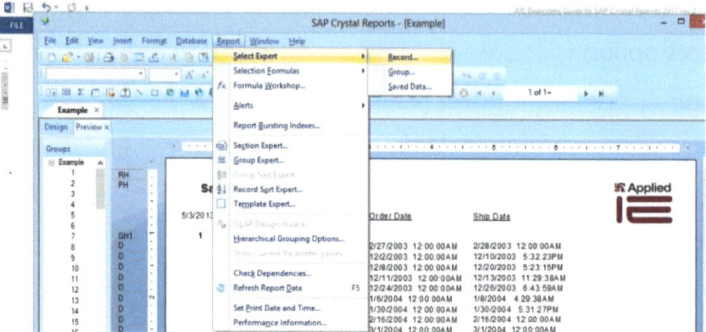

… Another approach is …

1. Click on **Select Expert icon** pull down menu
2. Select **Record**

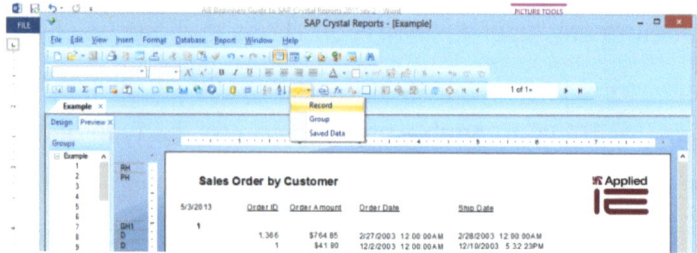

38

3. Select field *Orders.Order Amount* to filter
4. Select **OK**

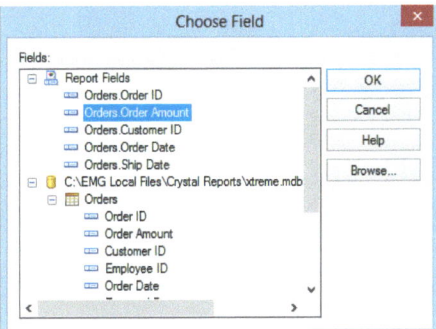

5. Select the filter command such as *is greater than*
6. Enter the value such as **1000**
7. Select **OK**

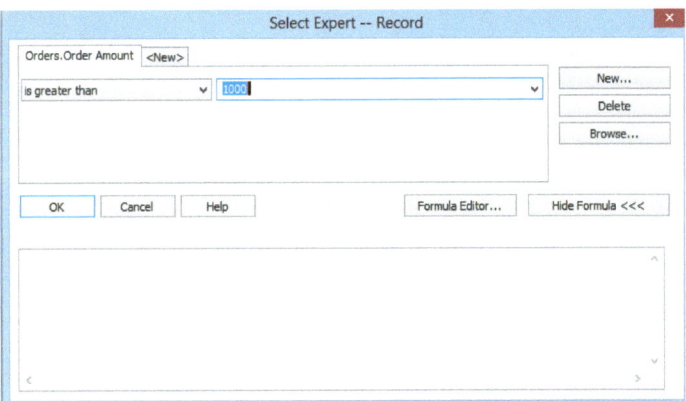

Report Filters and Parameters

8. Select **Use Saved Data** to view previously downloaded data or **Refresh Data** to download new set of data

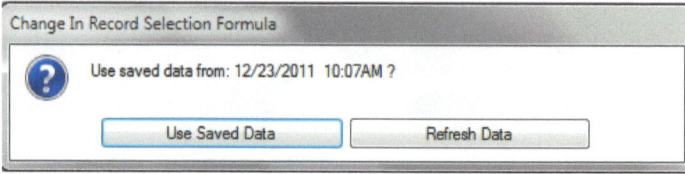

9. Select **Preview** to view report

Sales Order by Customer

5/3/2013	Order ID	Order Amount	Order Date	Ship Date
1				
	1,033	$3,520.30	12/8/2003 12:00:00AM	12/20/2003 5:23:15PM
	1,246	$3,884.25	1/30/2004 12:00:00AM	1/30/2004 5:31:27PM
	1,296	$6,682.98	2/16/2004 12:00:00AM	2/16/2004 12:00:00AM
	1,387	$1,515.35	3/1/2004 12:00:00AM	3/1/2004 12:00:00AM
	1,763	$2,378.35	6/24/2004 12:00:00AM	6/30/2004 12:00:00AM
	2,054	$4,078.95	9/1/2004 12:00:00AM	9/2/2004 12:00:00AM
	2,640	$2,939.85	1/26/2005 12:00:00AM	1/26/2005 12:00:00AM
	2,772	$2,294.55	2/28/2005 12:00:00AM	3/5/2005 12:00:00AM
	2,900	$5,549.40	4/9/2005 12:00:00AM	4/16/2005 12:00:00AM
2				
	1,303	$1,505.10	2/18/2003 12:00:00AM	3/2/2003 12:00:00AM
	1,254	$2,497.05	2/3/2004 12:00:00AM	2/4/2004 3:51:39PM
	1,288	$8,819.55	2/12/2004 12:00:00AM	2/12/2004 12:00:00AM
	1,633	$5,879.70	5/21/2004 12:00:00AM	5/23/2004 12:00:00AM
	1,743	$1,489.05	6/20/2004 12:00:00AM	6/23/2004 12:00:00AM
	1,883	$3,526.70	7/21/2004 12:00:00AM	7/27/2004 12:00:00AM
	1,916	$1,131.25	7/29/2004 12:00:00AM	7/30/2004 12:00:00AM
	1,915	$1,086.05	7/29/2004 12:00:00AM	8/3/2004 12:00:00AM
	1,941	$5,879.70	8/6/2004 12:00:00AM	8/14/2004 12:00:00AM
	2,243	$1,523.35	10/19/2004 12:00:00AM	10/19/2004 12:00:00AM
	2,242	$8,819.55	10/19/2004 12:00:00AM	10/19/2004 12:00:00AM
	2,606	$1,083.04	1/15/2005 12:00:00AM	1/15/2005 12:00:00AM
	2,652	$2,429.10	1/29/2005 12:00:00AM	2/5/2005 12:00:00AM
	2,653	$2,451.85	1/29/2005 12:00:00AM	2/8/2005 12:00:00AM
	2,777	$1,529.70	3/1/2005 12:00:00AM	3/8/2005 12:00:00AM
	2,969	$3,185.42	4/26/2005 12:00:00AM	5/1/2005 12:00:00AM

Creating Parameter Fields

1. Open Field Explorer

2. Right-Mouse click Parameter Fields

3. Select **New**

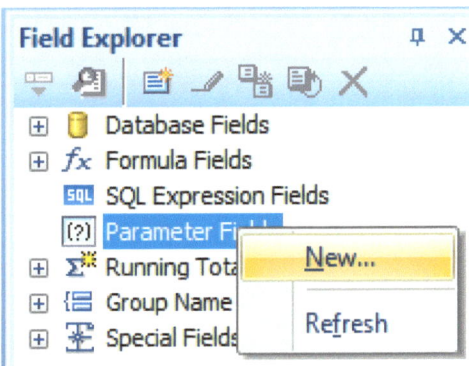

4. Enter Name of the Parameter field

5. Select the parameter **Type** to match the data field type. See Tip: Browse Data

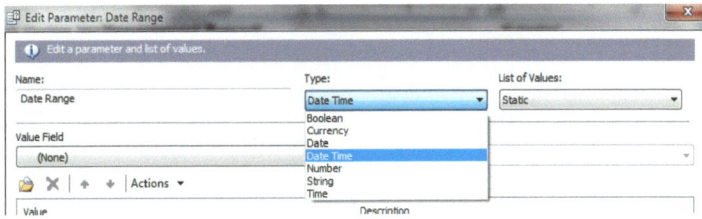

6. For a date range, select **Option: Allow Range Values** to **True**

7. Select **OK**

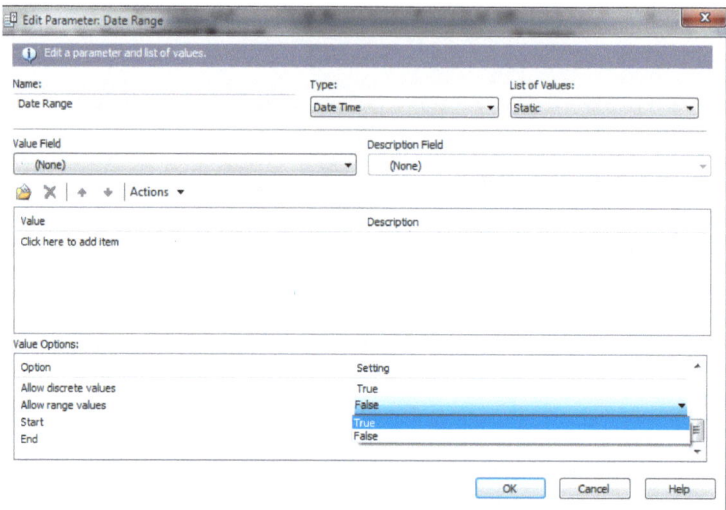

Beginner's Guide to Crystal Reports 2011

Setting Up a Report Parameter

1. Select **Report**
2. Click on **Select Expert**
3. Select **Record**

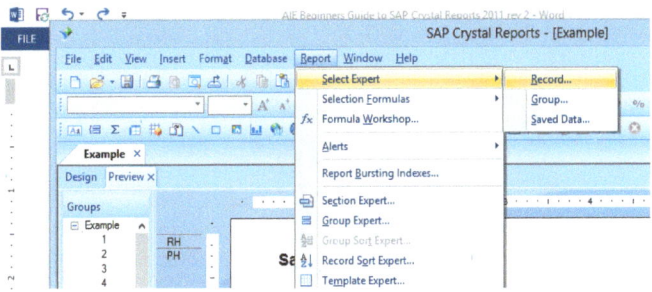

4. Select **New** Tab
5. Select field *Orders.Order Date* to set parameter
6. Select **OK**

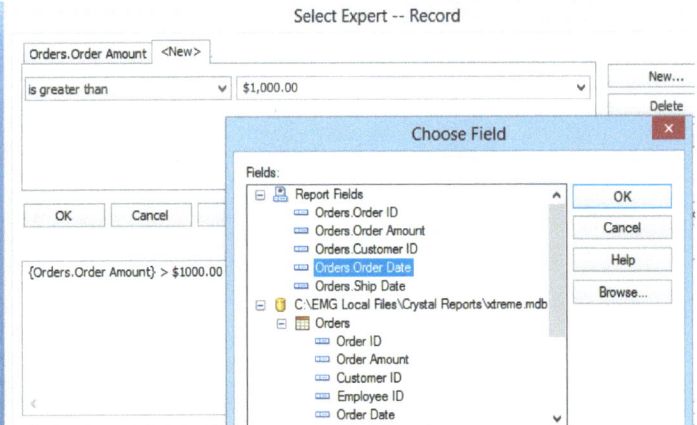

7. Set condition to "**is equal to**"

8. Go to pull-down menu to select user created parameter field that starts with a "**?**". If you do not find the parameter field, the parameter field does not have the same field type as the selected field. Go to the parameter field and change the field type.

9. Select **OK** to save

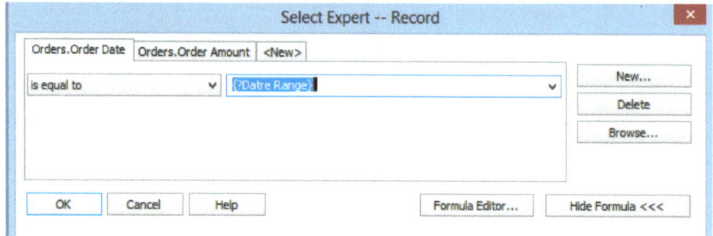

10. Select **Preview** to view or run report

11. Pop-up menu appears for the parameter range

12. Enter **Date** or use the calendar icon to select the start and end dates

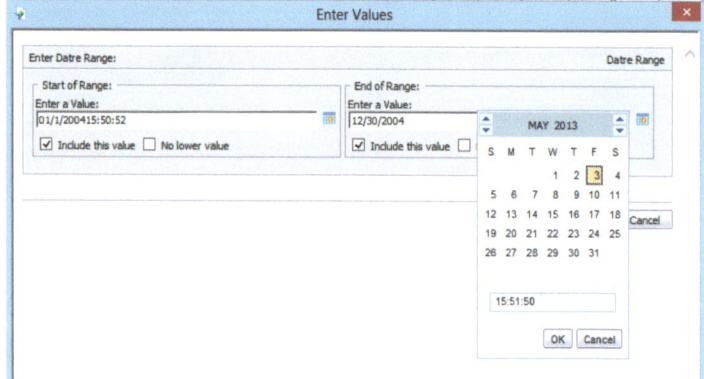

TIP: Browse Data

Examine the *Field Type* and *Browse Data* to learn more about the data set in a field.

1. Open **Field Explorer**
2. Right-Mouse click on the field
3. Select **Browse Data**

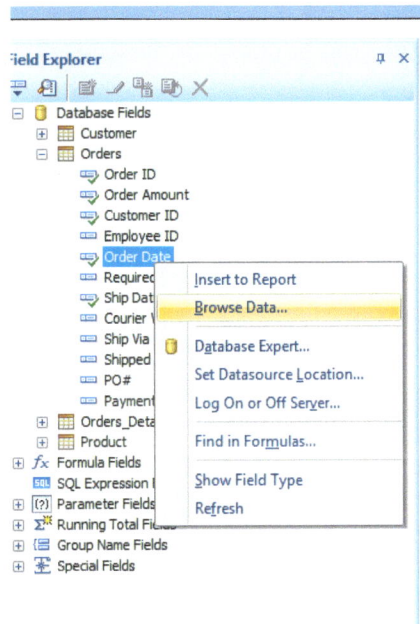

Report Filters and Parameters

4. View sample data

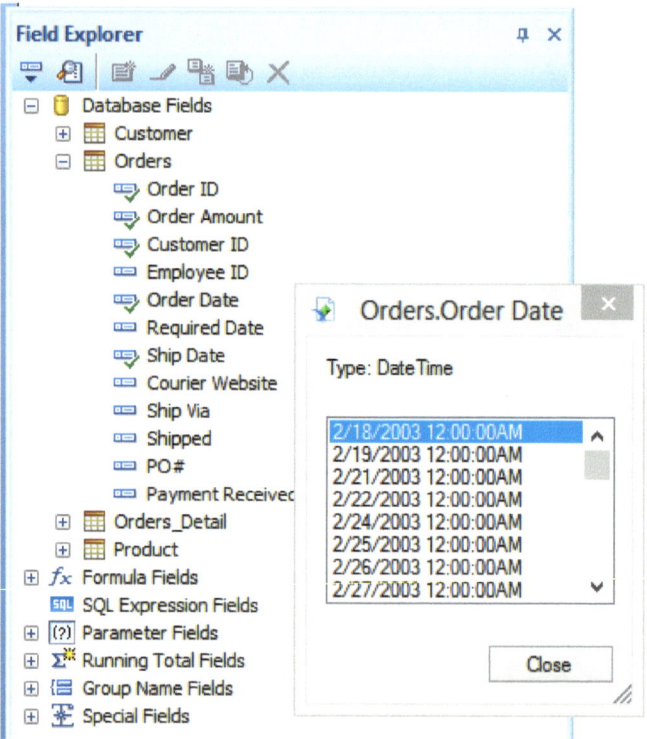

Chapter 6: Basic Math Functions

Adding Field Data with Running Totals Fields

Creating a Running Total Field

1. Open the **Field Explorer**
2. Right-Mouse click Running Totals Fields
3. Select **New**

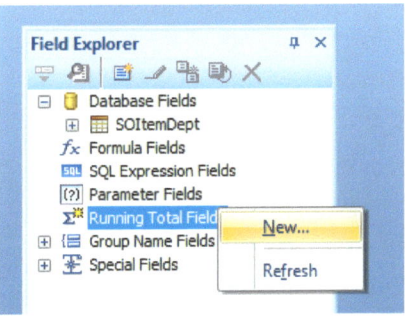

4. Type the **Running Total Name**
5. Click on the field *Orders.Order Amount*
6. Click the ">" icon to select the field name
7. Select the "Type of Summary" such as *sum*

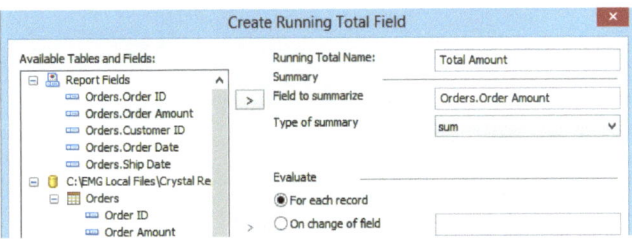

Basic Math Functions

8. For the **Reset** option, select **On Change of Group**

9. Select **OK** when done

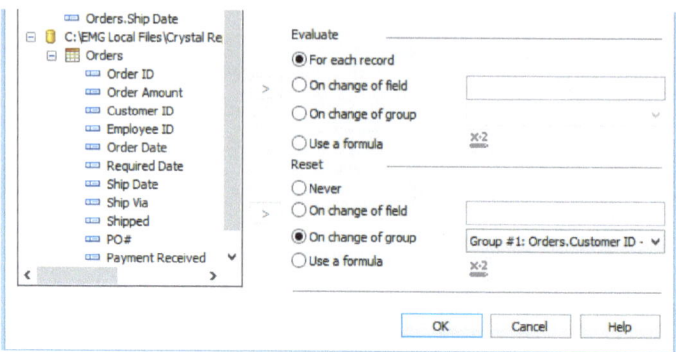

10. Notice the new field under Running Total Fields

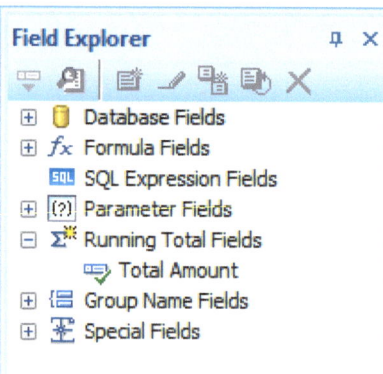

Inserting a Running Total Field

1. Drag the running total field in the Group Footer #1 section

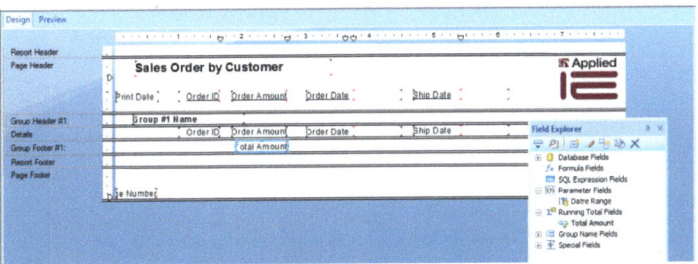

2. Select **Preview** to view report

Basic Math Functions

Adding Formula Fields

Creating a Formula Filed

1. Open **Field Explorer**

2. Right-Mouse click Formula Fields

3. Select **New**

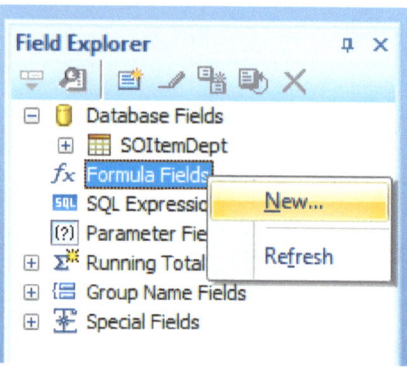

4. Enter Formula Name such as *Exchange $*

5. Select **OK**

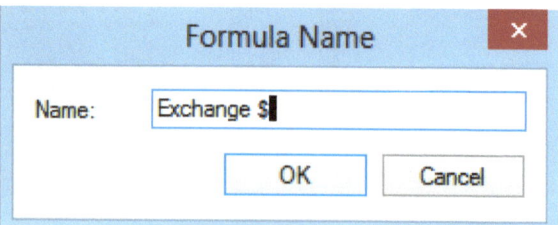

6. Type the "**{**" to display the table options

7. Select the table **Order**

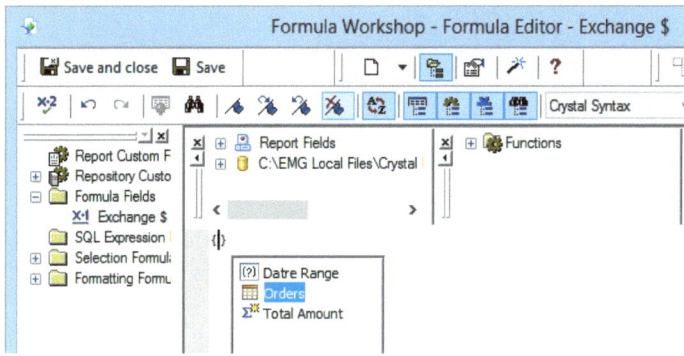

8. Select the field **Amount**

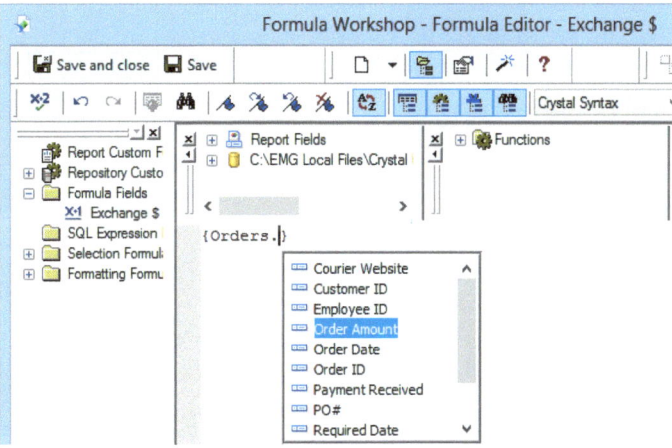

Basic Math Functions

9. Type the math operation **{Order.Amount) * 5**

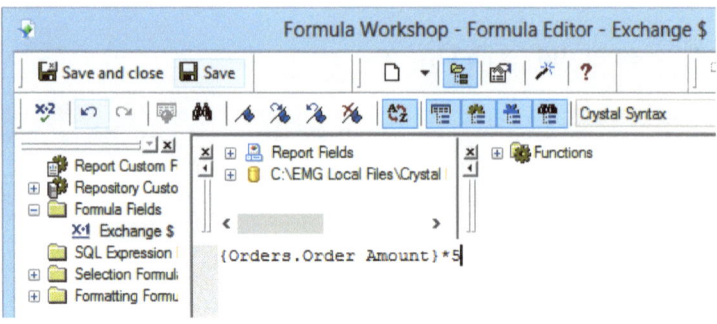

10. Select the [X-2] icon or **Alt-C** to verify formula
11. Select **OK**
12. Select **Save and Close**

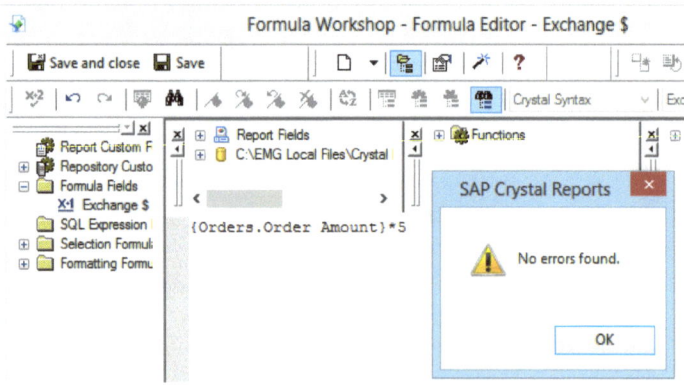

13. Notice the new field under the Formula Fields

Sales Order by Customer

	Order ID	Order Amount	Order Date	Ship Date
1				
	1,246	$3,884.25	01/30/2004	01/30/2004
	1,296	$6,682.98	02/16/2004	02/16/2004
	1,387	$1,515.35	03/01/2004	03/01/2004
	1,763	$2,378.35	06/24/2004	06/30/2004
	2,054	$4,078.95	09/01/2004	09/02/2004
		$18,539.88		
2				
	1,254	$2,497.05	02/03/2004	02/04/2004
	1,288	$8,819.55	02/12/2004	02/12/2004
	1,633	$5,879.70	05/21/2004	05/23/2004
	1,743	$1,489.05	06/20/2004	06/23/2004
	1,883	$3,526.70	07/21/2004	07/27/2004
	1,916	$1,131.25	07/29/2004	07/30/2004
	1,915	$1,086.05	07/29/2004	08/03/2004

Field Explorer
- Database Fields
  - Orders
- Formula Fields
  - Exchange $
- SQL Expression Fields
- Parameter Fields
  - Datre Range
- Running Total Fields
  - Total Amount
- Group Name Fields
- Special Fields

Basic Math Functions

Inserting a Formula Field

1. Select and drag the formula field **Exchange $** in the Details section

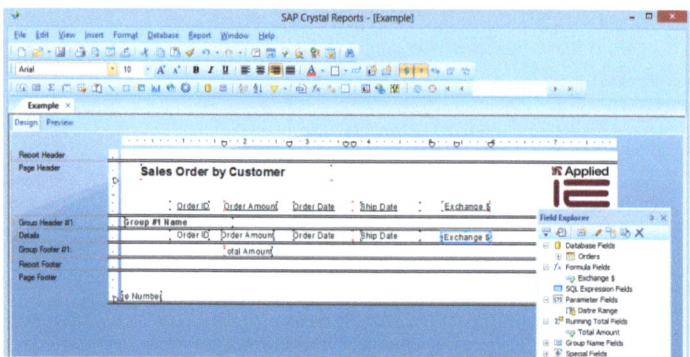

2. Select **Preview** tab to view report

Sales Order by Customer

	Order ID	Order Amount	Order Date	Ship Date	Exchange $
1					
	1,246	$3,884.25	01/30/2004	01/30/2004	$19,421.25
	1,296	$6,682.98	02/16/2004	02/16/2004	$33,414.90
	1,387	$1,515.35	03/01/2004	03/01/2004	$7,576.75
	1,763	$2,378.35	06/24/2004	06/30/2004	$11,891.75
	2,054	$4,078.95	09/01/2004	09/02/2004	$20,394.75
		$18,539.88			
2					
	1,254	$2,497.05	02/03/2004	02/04/2004	$12,485.25
	1,288	$8,819.55	02/12/2004	02/12/2004	$44,097.75
	1,633	$5,879.70	05/21/2004	05/23/2004	$29,398.50
	1,743	$1,489.05	06/20/2004	06/23/2004	$7,445.25
	1,883	$3,526.70	07/21/2004	07/27/2004	$17,633.50
	1,916	$1,131.25	07/29/2004	07/30/2004	$5,656.25
	1,915	$1,086.05	07/29/2004	08/03/2004	$5,430.25
	1,941	$5,879.70	08/06/2004	08/14/2004	$29,398.50
	2,243	$1,523.35	10/19/2004	10/19/2004	$7,616.75
	2,242	$8,819.55	10/19/2004	10/19/2004	$44,097.75
		$40,651.95			
3					
	1,294	$5,879.70	02/15/2004	02/15/2004	$29,398.50
	1,357	$1,664.70	02/26/2004	02/26/2004	$8,323.50
	1,964	$1,721.25	08/12/2004	08/13/2004	$8,606.25
	2,112	$5,545.42	09/16/2004	09/24/2004	$27,727.10
	2,162	$1,019.70	09/28/2004	09/30/2004	$5,098.50
		$15,830.77			

Chapter 7: Summary Reports

Creating a Summary Report

Reports can be developed to show summaries, such as the totals and averages, for a certain time period or grouping of data. Report developers can provide access to users to "drill-down" and show the details of each summary.

Hiding Report Details with Drill Down

1. Right-Mouse click the Details section

2. Select **Hide (Drill-Down OK)**. Select **Suppress (No Drill Down)** to disable drill-down option

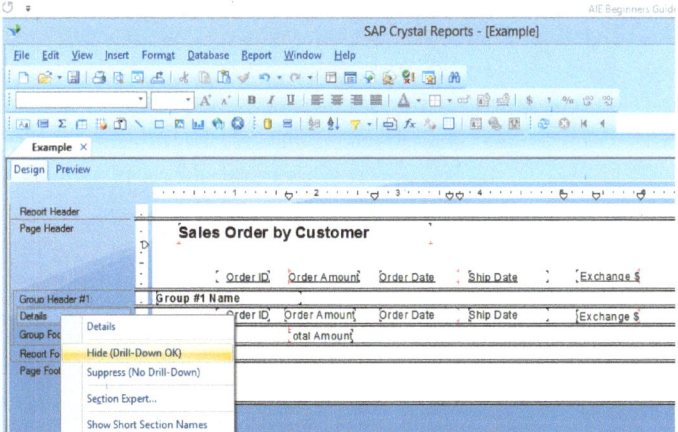

Summary Reports

3. Select **Preview** tab to view report

Sales Order by Customer

	Order ID	Order Amount	Order Date	Ship Date	Exchange $
1		$18,539.88			
2		$40,651.95			
3		$15,830.77			
4		$62,905.99			
5					

4. Double-click on Department name to Drill-Down or view details of summary

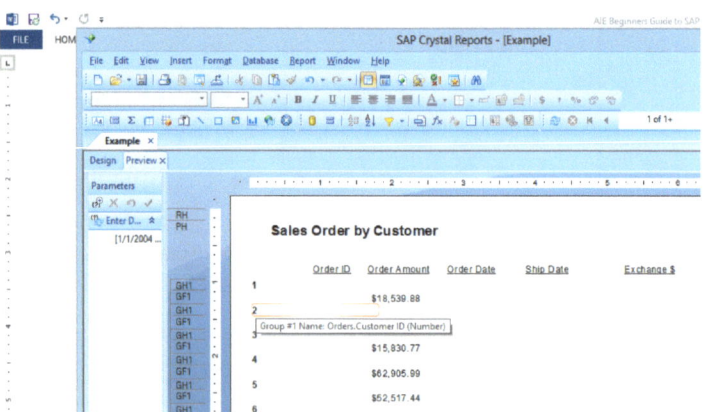

5. Notice a new tab with the drill-down results

6. Select "**x**" on the details tab to close the view

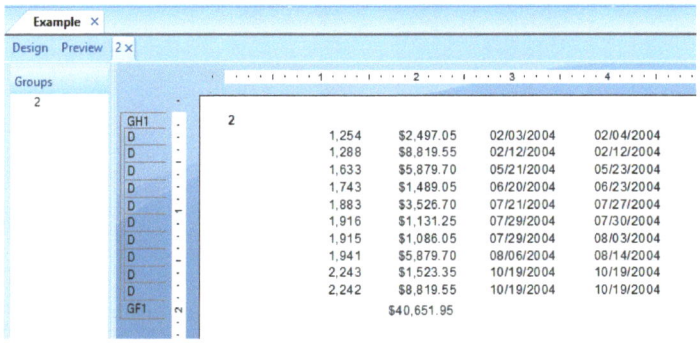

Refining the Summary Report

1. Click on Design tab

2. Move the Group Field Name from the Group Header section to the Group Footer section

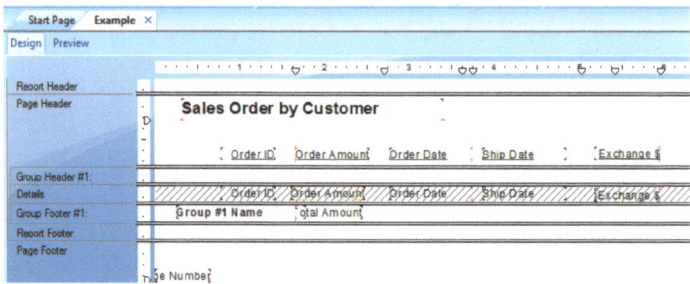

3. Move the field titles or column header from the Page Header section to the Group Header section

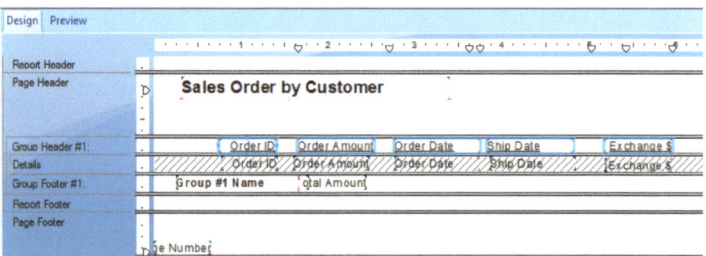

4. Copy the "Order Amount" text

    a. Right-click on the text

    b. Select Copy

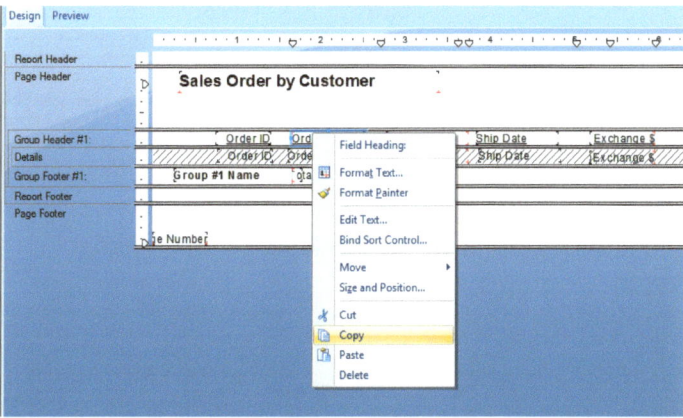

5. Paste "Order Amount" text to the Page Header section

    a. Right-mouse click on the Page Header section

    b. Select Paste

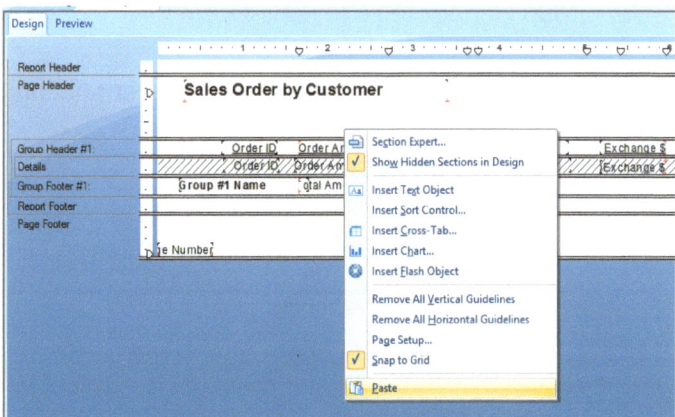

6. Position "Order Amount" text

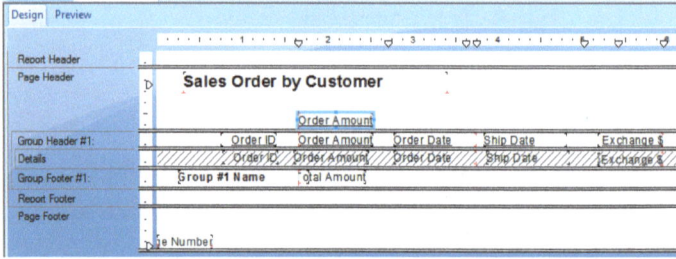

7. Add "Customer ID" text to label column header

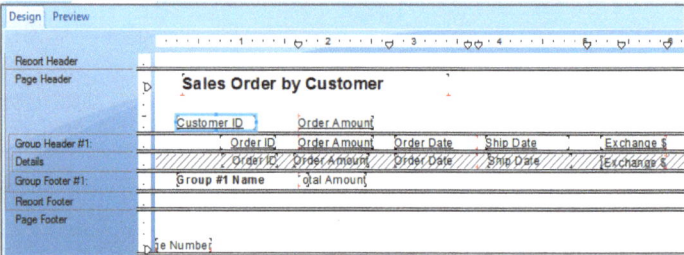

8. Set Group Header to Hide (Drill-Down OK)

    a. Right-mouse click on Group Header section

    b. Select Hide (Drill-Down OK)

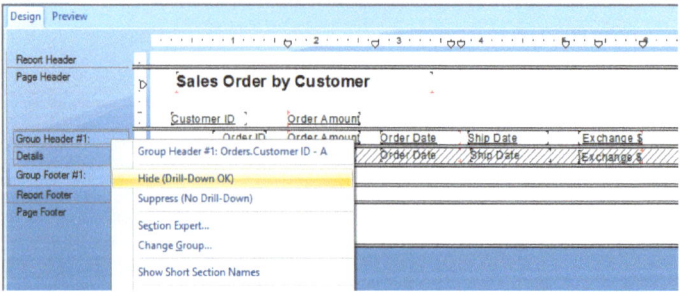

9. Select Preview tab

Sales Order by Customer

Customer ID	Order Amount
1	$18,539.88
2	$40,651.95
3	$15,830.77
4	$62,905.99
5	$52,517.44
6	$36,343.95
7	$15,777.99
8	$14,666.16
9	$21,888.09
10	$26,569.08
11	$32,857.62
12	$45,771.49
13	$27,542.57
14	$23,014.10
15	$27,434.90

10. Double-click on Customer ID record to view details

Order ID	Order Amount	Order Date	Ship Date	Exchange $
1,254	$2,497.05	02/03/2004	02/04/2004	$12,485.25
1,288	$8,819.55	02/12/2004	02/12/2004	$44,097.75
1,633	$5,879.70	05/21/2004	05/23/2004	$29,398.50
1,743	$1,489.05	06/20/2004	06/23/2004	$7,445.25
1,883	$3,526.70	07/21/2004	07/27/2004	$17,633.50
1,916	$1,131.25	07/29/2004	07/30/2004	$5,656.25
1,915	$1,086.05	07/29/2004	08/03/2004	$5,430.25
1,941	$5,879.70	08/06/2004	08/14/2004	$29,398.50
2,243	$1,523.35	10/19/2004	10/19/2004	$7,616.75
2,242	$8,819.55	10/19/2004	10/19/2004	$44,097.75
	$40,651.95			

2

Summary Reports

Chapter 8: Using Multiple Data Tables

Identifying Data Tables Required for a Report

1. Create a pencil draft of the proposed report to create
2. Identify the data fields required for the report
3. Determine if the fields can be found in a single data table in the Tables or Views
4. Identify the tables containing the required data fields
5. Identify common data fields to link or connect multiple data fields. These common fields are also known as key fields

Selecting Data Tables

1. Select **File**
2. Select **New**
3. Select **Standard Report**

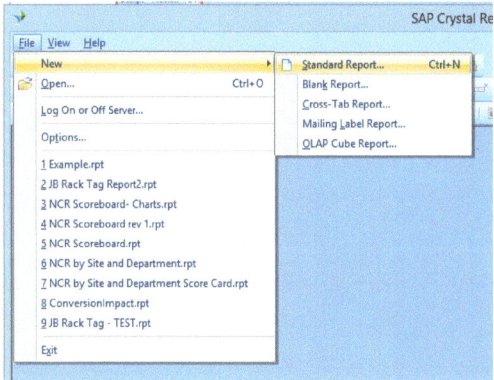

Using Multiple Data Tables

4. Select **Data Source**
5. Expand to the table location
6. Expand to view tables

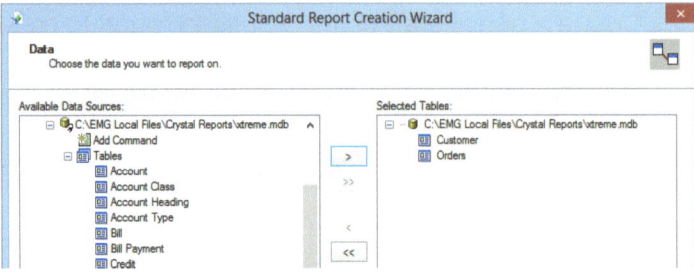

7. Select tables **Orders** and **Customer**
8. Click on **Next**
9. Verify the field links of the tables. The automatic detection of linking fields require user review.
10. Select **Finish**

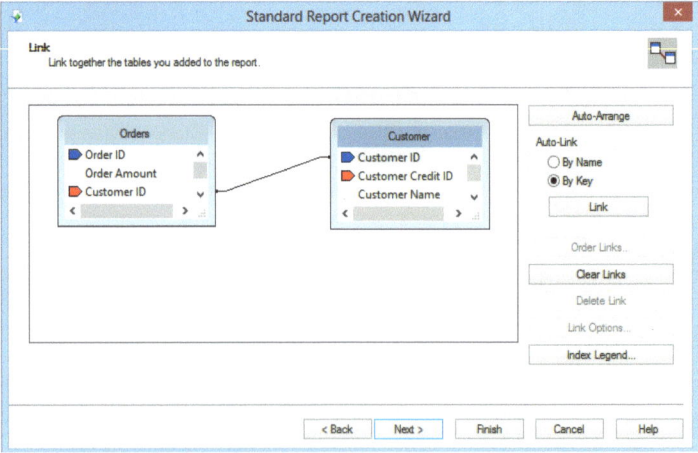

Linking Fields

Common key fields are required to link tables as shown below. In some cases, there may be multiple key fields that are required to logically connect tables.

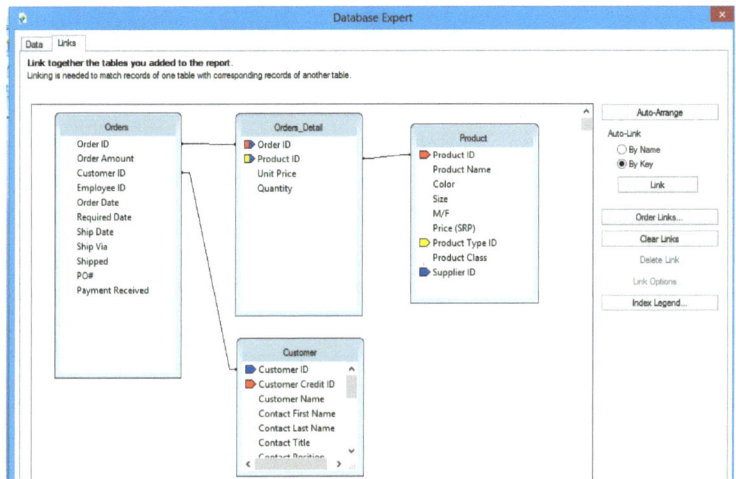

Color-coded markings next to key fields indicate the indexing priority of the table. As much as possible, select indexed fields for quicker data access.

Using Multiple Data Tables

Chapter 9: Adding a Chart

Creating the Basic Chart

1. Click on the **Design** tab

2. Expand the **Report Footer** to allocate space for a chart

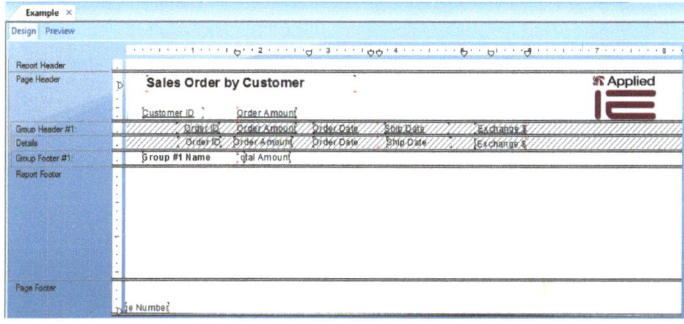

3. Select **Insert**

4. Select **Chart**

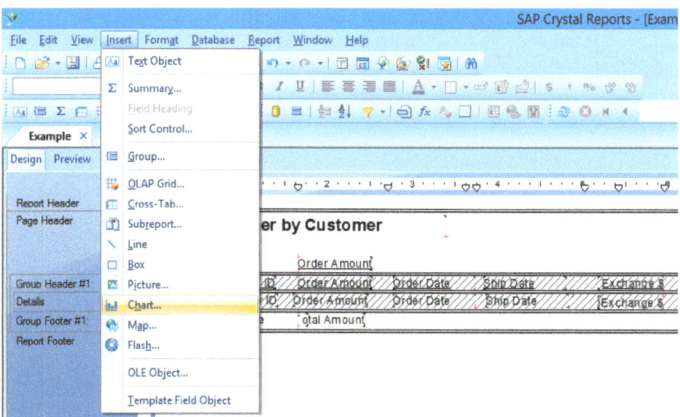

Adding a Chart

5. Aim and click guide box at Page Footer even if the box is larger than the allocated space

6. Select **Orders.Ship_Date**

7. Click on ">" next to **On change of**

8. Select the Running Totals formula **Total Amount**

9. Click on ">" next to **Show value(s)**

10. Select **OK**

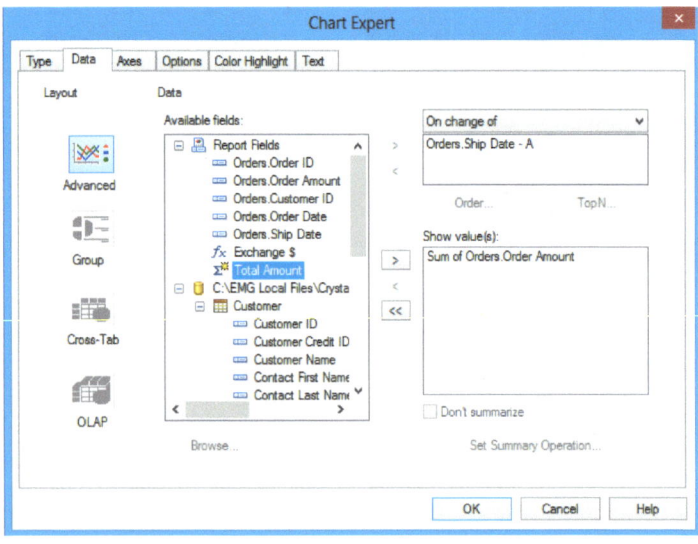

11. Select Preview

12. Go to last page Report Footer to view chart

    Notice the chart displaying the total Order Amount per ship date with a Legend Box on the right.

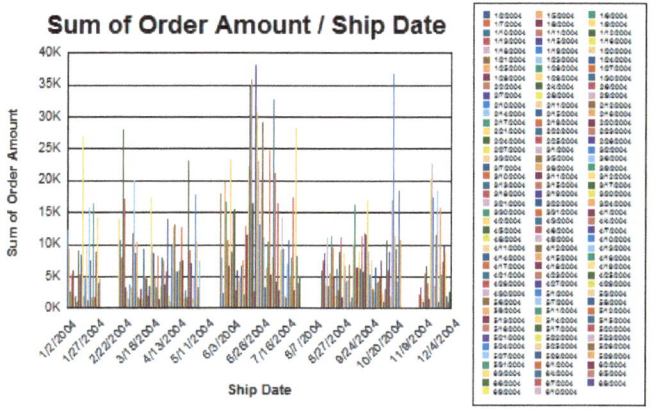

Changing Daily Amount to a Monthly Amount

1. Right-mouse click on chart to display menu

2. Select **Chart Expert**

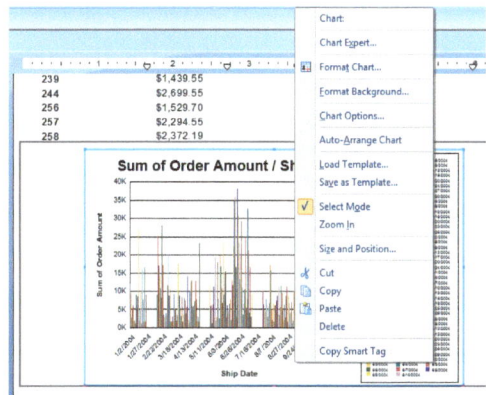

Adding a Chart

3. Select **Data** tab

4. Select On change of field **Orders.Ship_Date**

5. Change **The section will be printed:** option from **for each day** to **for each month**

6. Select **OK**

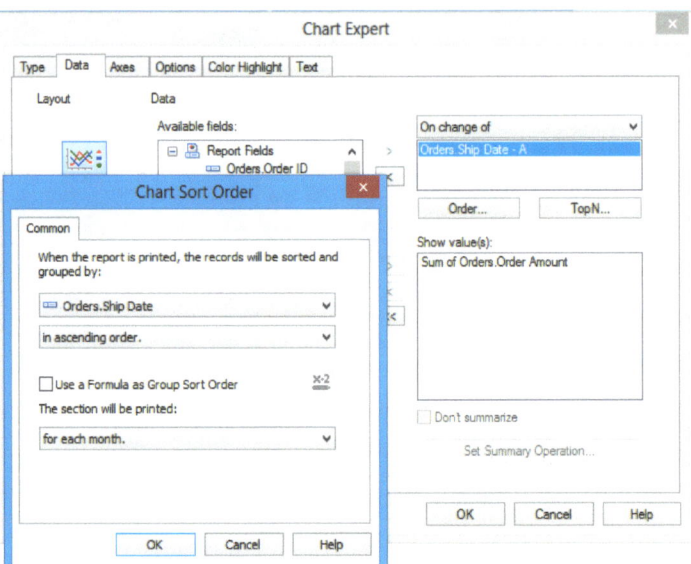

7. Chart displays Total Order Amount per Month

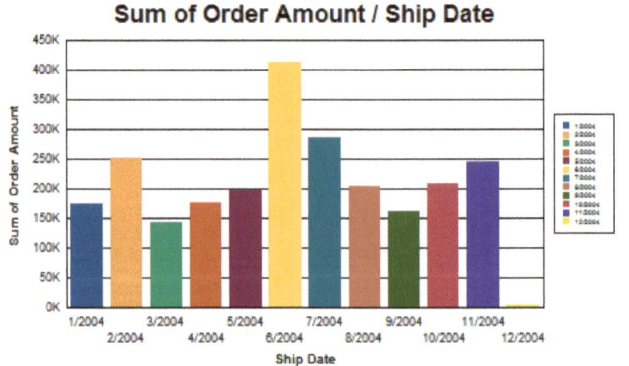

Removing the Legend Box

1. Right-mouse click on the chart area to display the menu

2. Select Chart Expert

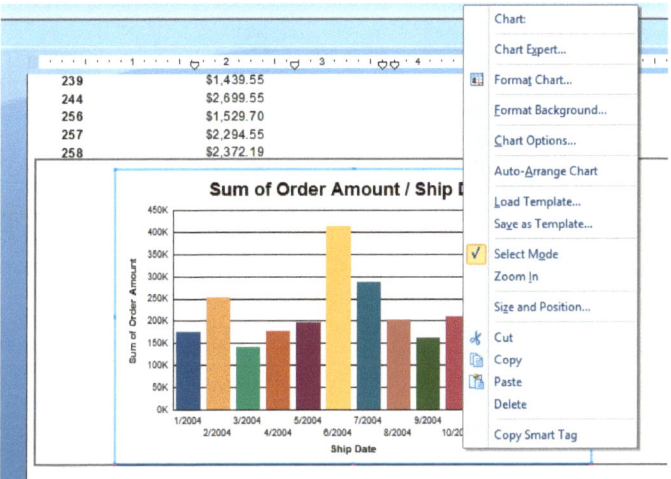

3. Select **Options** tab

4. Unselect or uncheck the **Show Legend** box

5. Select **OK**

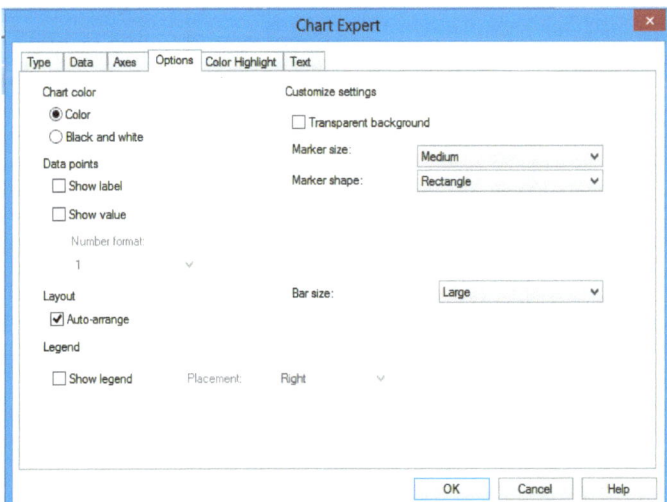

Adding a Chart

6. View the chart without the Legend Box.

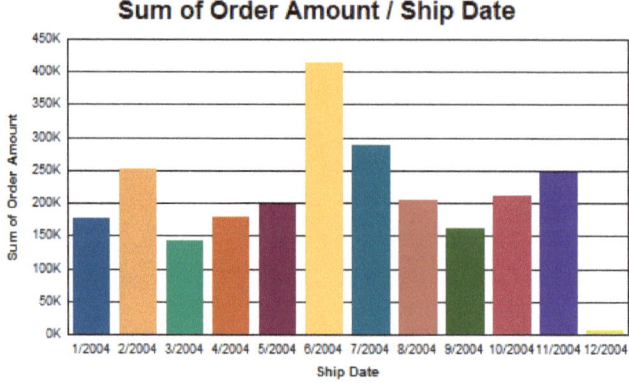

Changing Titles and Labels

1. Right-mouse click on the chart area to display the menu
2. Select **Chart Expert**

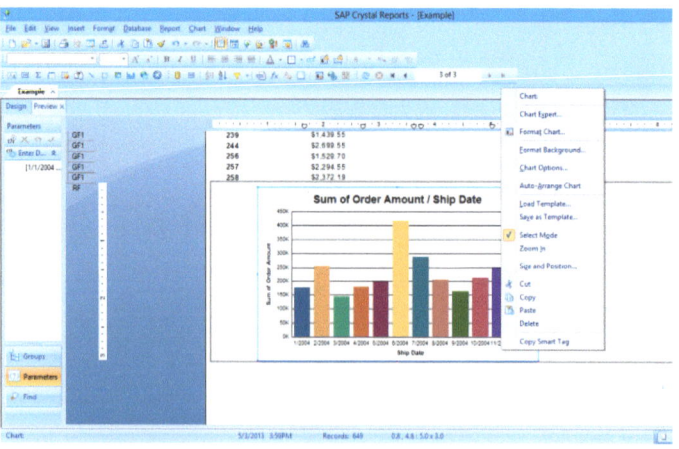

3. Select the **Text** tab

4. Uncheck the applicable **Auto-Text** check box

5. Enter the titles and labels

6. Select OK

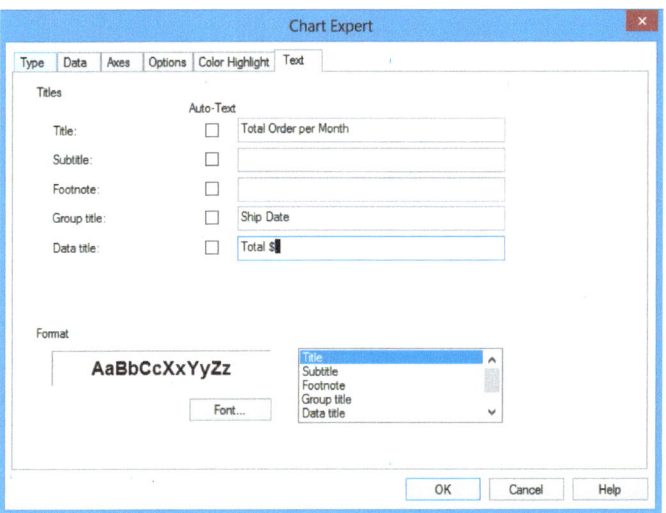

7. View the updated chart

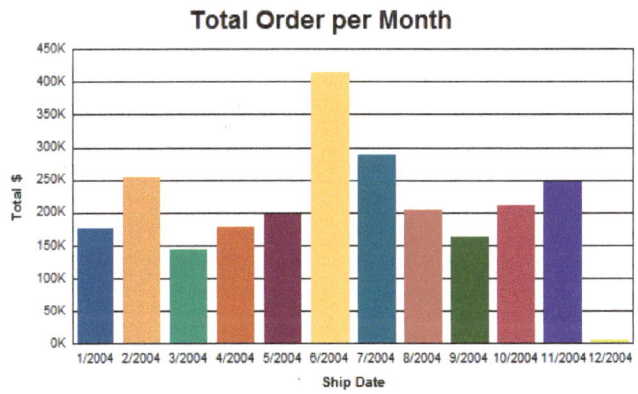

Adding a Chart

Changing the Chart Type

1. Right-mouse click on the chart area to display the menu
2. Select **Chart Expert**
3. At the Type tab, select **Line** and the appropriate Line Chart type
4. Select **OK**

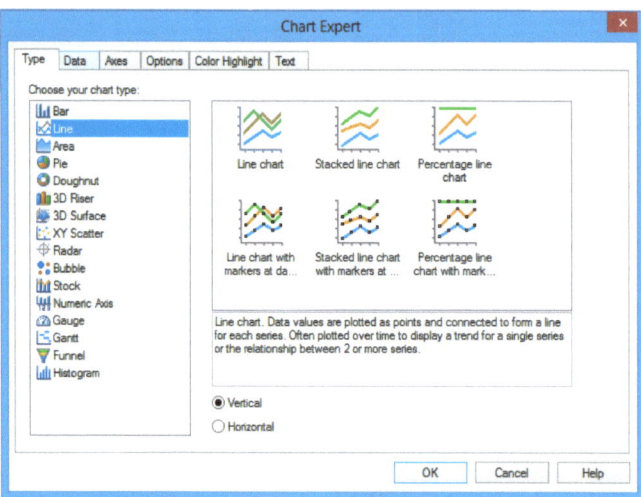

5. View the updated chart

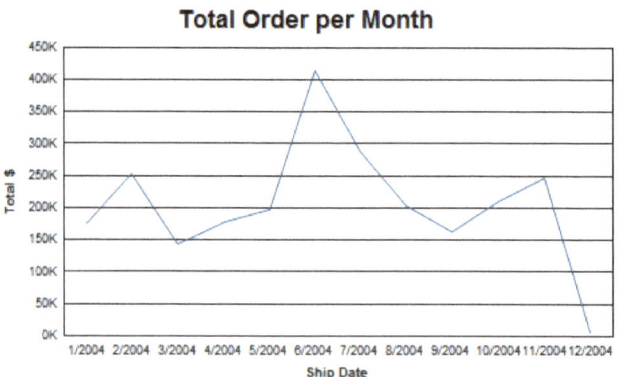

Chapter 10: Cross-Tabs

Cross Tab is an easy-to-use utility to create a detailed data grid or a summary data grid.

Creating a Cross-Tab

1. Select **Insert** menu
2. Select **Cross-Tab**

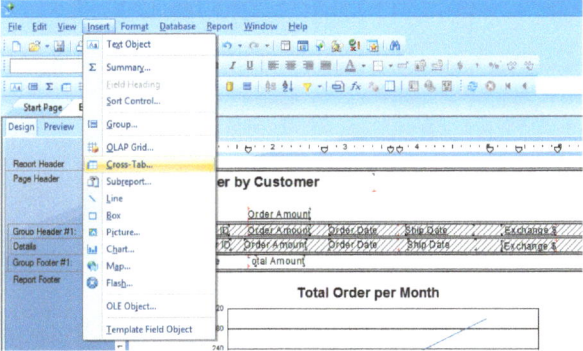

3. Position and click guide box to position Cross-Tab
4. Right-mouse click on Cross-Tab to open menu
5. Select **Cross-Tab Expert**

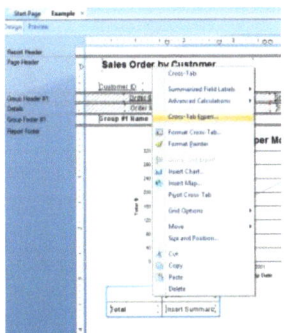

Data Grids Using Cross Tabs

6. Select **Orders.Order_Date**
7. Select ">" on Rows
8. Select **Total Amount formula**
9. Select ">" on Summary Fields

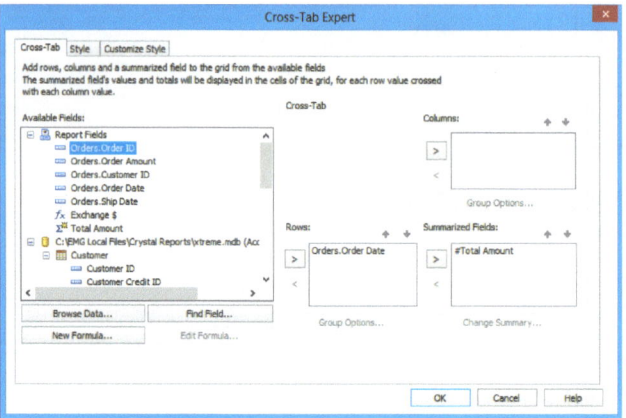

10. Select **Preview**

    Notice that the Total Amount listed by day

	Total
Total	$4,317,395.77
1/2/2004	$3,842.55
1/5/2004	$2,654.56
1/6/2004	$1,830.35
1/8/2004	$5,879.70

Summarizing Data

1. Right-mouse click on Cross-Tab to open menu
2. Select **Cross-Tab Expert**

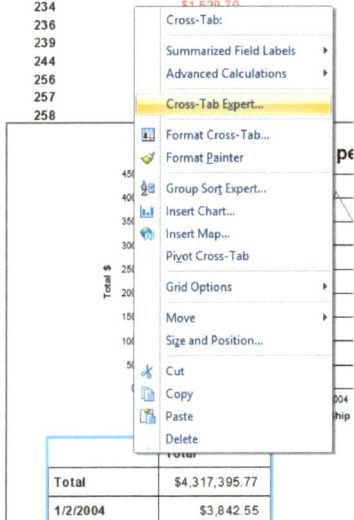

3. Click on **Orders.Order_Date**
4. Select **Group Option**
5. Click on **Row will be printed** pull down menu
6. Select summary period such as **for each month**

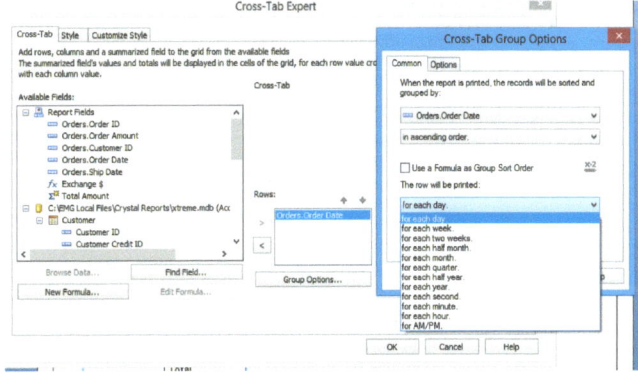

7. Select **OK** on Cross-Tab Group Options
8. Select **OK** on Cross-Tab Expert to view result

	Total
Total	$159,569.76
1/2004	$1,409.55
2/2004	$2,416.80
3/2004	$5,952.85
4/2004	$4,288.90

Adding Data Columns

1. Right-mouse click on Cross-Tab to open menu
2. Select **Cross-Tab Expert**

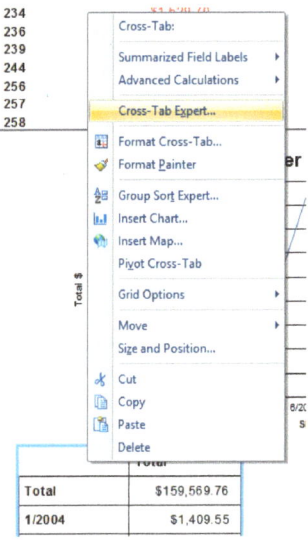

3. Select **Orders.Customer_ID**
4. Select "**>**" on Columns

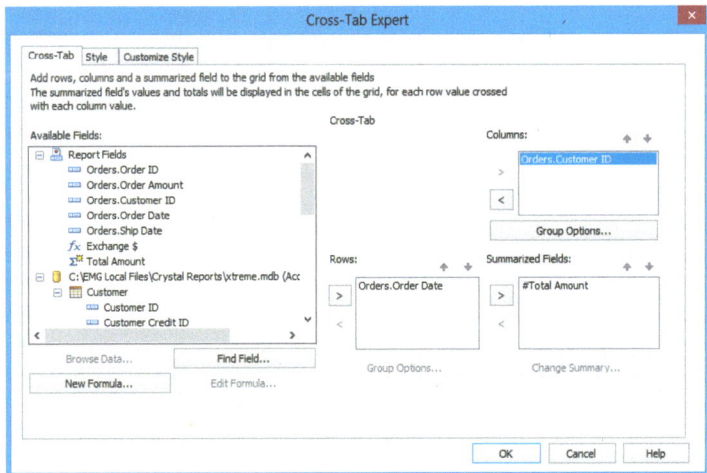

5. Select OK to view result. The cross-tab shows total monthly amount per customer ID.

	Total	1	2	3	4	5
Total	$8,051,160.91	$18,539.88	$40,651.95	$15,830.77	$62,905.99	$52,517.44
1/2004	$195,117.54	$3,884.25	$0.00	$0.00	$0.00	$11,792.66
2/2004	$309,780.53	$10,567.23	$11,316.60	$7,544.40	$0.00	$28,675.52
3/2004	$331,301.39	$12,082.58	$0.00	$0.00	$3,147.21	$34,439.44
4/2004	$387,327.71	$0.00	$0.00	$0.00	$18,716.16	$0.00

Chapter 11: Intermediate Skills and Tips

This chapter is a collection of commonly used features for intermediate users of Crystal Reports®. It is recommended that readers be proficient on the fundamental skills described in Chapters 1 to 9 prior to reading this chapter.

Parameter Field Options

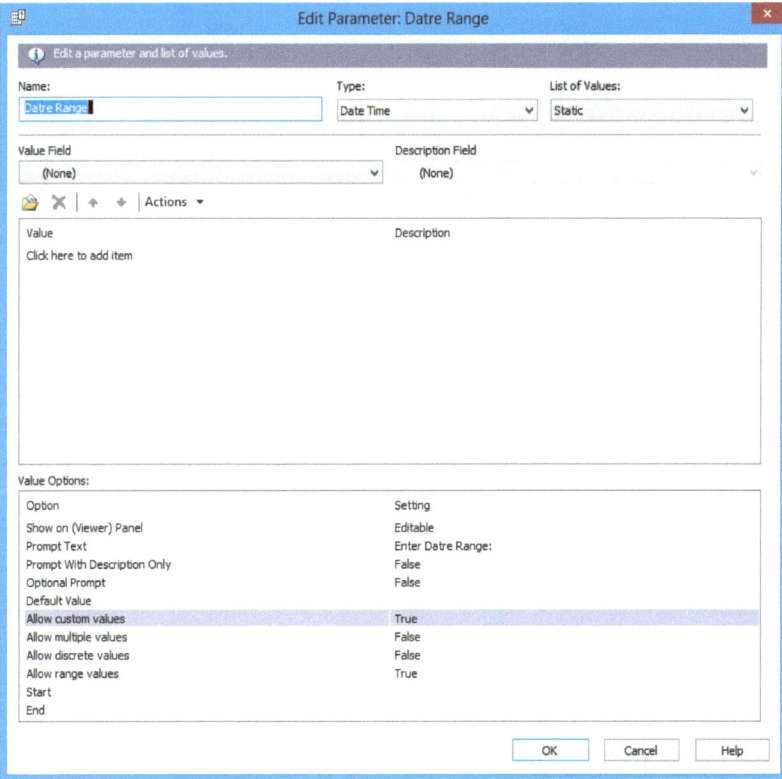

Intermediate Skills and Tips

Value Field

Introduction Use this option to create a Pick List of items for a report user.

Options
1. Select Value Field
2. Select Actions
3. Select Append all database values

Value Options

Prompt Text Option to change the default message

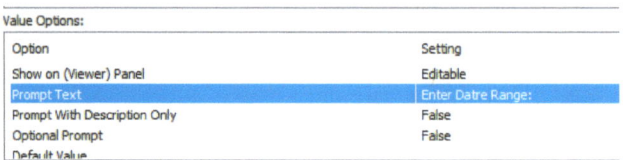

Default Value Option to set a default value for the user.

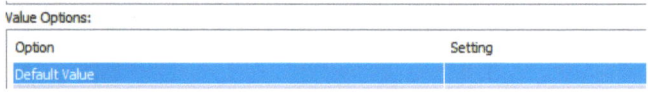

Allow Multiple Values Option for the user to select multiple values from a pick list or enter the values manually.

Set Allow Multiple Values = True

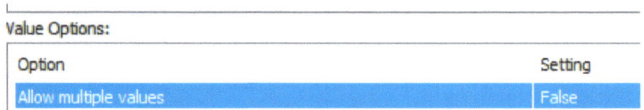

Allow Range Values Option for the user to enter a minimum and maximum value. Set Allow range values = True

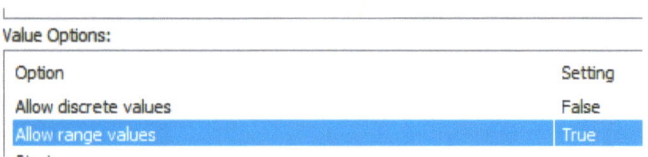

Beginner's Guide to Crystal Reports 2011

Change Date-Time parameter to Date Only

Introduction Setting up a parameter requires the field type to be the same as the field used in Select Expert. With a Time parameter included, there is risk of excluding data in a date range prompt. Changing the parameter from Date-Time to Date assures complete data extraction and simplifies the Date Range prompt.

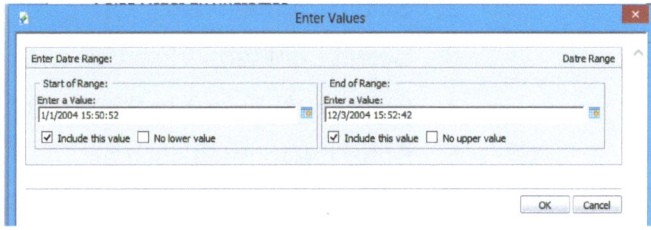

Procedure
1. Set up the parameter field to match the Date-Time field type
2. Add the data field and parameter field in **Select Expert**
3. Edit the Parameter field Type from Date-Time to **Date**

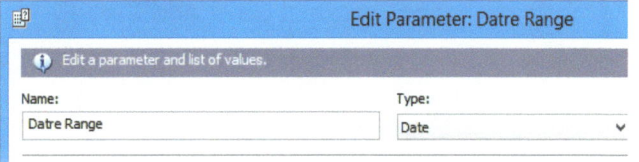

4. Change the **Allow Range Values** = True
5. Select OK

Result

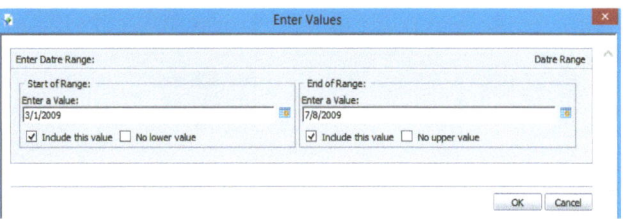

83

Intermediate Skills and Tips

Field Format

Change Font Color Based on a Formula Condition

Introduction   The font color can be changed when a certain condition in a formula is satisfied.

Procedure
1. Right-mouse click on field to show menu
2. Select Format Field
3. Select Font tab
4. Click on [X-2] icon to the right of Color:
5. Enter the formula such as

    If {#Total Amount}<20000 then crRed else crBlack

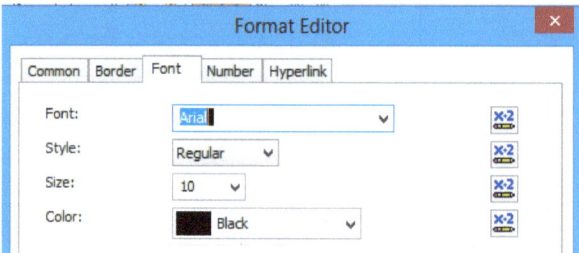

6. Select Save and Close
7. Select OK

Result

Sales Order by Customer

Customer ID	Order Amount
1	$18,539.88
2	$40,651.95
3	$15,830.77
4	$62,905.99
5	$52,517.44
6	$36,343.95
7	$15,777.99
8	$14,666.16
9	$21,888.09

Suppressing a Field Value

Introduction — A formula or a data field can be suppressed, or not be displayed, based on a set parameter.

Procedure
1. Right-mouse click on field to show menu
2. Select Format Field
3. Select Common tab
4. Click on [X-2] icon to the right of the Suppress checkbox
5. Enter the formula such as

    {#Total Amount}<20000

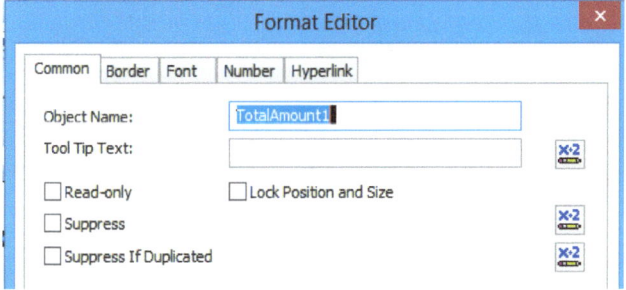

6. Select Save and Close
7. Select OK

Result

Sales Order by Customer

Customer ID	Order Amount
1	
2	$40,651.95
3	
4	$62,905.99
5	$52,517.44
6	$36,343.95
7	
8	
9	$21,888.09
10	$26,569.08
11	$32,857.62
12	$45,771.49

Formulas

Adding Text Fields

Syntax   {TableName.Fieldname1} + {TableName.FieldName2}

Example   If   {TableName.Fieldname1} = "John"
            {TableName.FieldName2} = "Smith"

Result   JohnSmith

Adding Text Fields and Fixed Characters

Syntax   {TableName.Fieldname1} + "-" +{TableName.FieldName2}

Example   If   {TableName.Fieldname1} = "John"
            {TableName.FieldName2} = "Smith"

Result   John-Smith

Converting a Number Field to Text

Syntax ToText (x, y, z)

x = {TableName.Fieldname}
y = Decimal Positions such as 0, 1, 2,...
z = Thousands separator such as a ","

Example If {TableName.Fieldname} = 1234.56

(1) ToText ({TableName.Fieldname},1,",")
(2) ToText ({TableName.Fieldname},0,"")

Result
(1) 1,234.5
(2) 1234

Selecting the First or Last Few Characters of a Field

Syntax Left (x,y)
Right (x,y)

x = {TableName.Fieldname}
y = Number of characters to extract

Example If {TableName.Fieldname} = "ABC123DEF45"

(1) Left ({TableName.Fieldname},4)
(2) Right ({TableName.Fieldname},3)

Result
(1) ABC1
(2) F45

Extracting a Numerical Value from a Date Field

Syntax DatePart (w, x)

w = Interval Type

x = {TableName.Fieldname}

Interval type value	Description
yyyy	Year value
q	Quarter value 1, 2, 3 or 4
m	Month value 1 to 12
y	Day of year 1 to 365 or 366 in a leap year
d	Day of the month 1 to 31
w	Day of week value 1 to 7 with Sunday as Day 1 as the default
ww	Week value of year 1 to 53
h	Hour value 0 to 23
n	Minute value 0 to 59
s	Seconds value 0 to 59

Example If {TableName.Fieldname} = 10/02/2013 5:31:27PM

(1) DatePart("yyyy", {TableName.Fieldname})

(2) DatePart("q", {TableName.Fieldname})

(3) DatePart("m", {TableName.Fieldname})

Result (1) 2013

(2) 4

(3) 10

Splitting or Selecting a Segment of a Delimited Field

Introduction   A Delimited field is a single data field containing multiple data components separated by a character (delimiter) such as a "-" or "|"

Syntax   Split (x,y) [n]

x = {TableName.Fieldname}

y = Delimiter or separator character such as "-"

n = The data component starting from the left

Example   If   {TableName.Fieldname} = "AAA-BB-CCC"

(3) Split ({TableName.Fieldname},"-")[2]

(4) Split ({TableName.Fieldname},"-")[1]

Result   (3) BB

(4) AAA

Intermediate Skills and Tips

Running Total Field

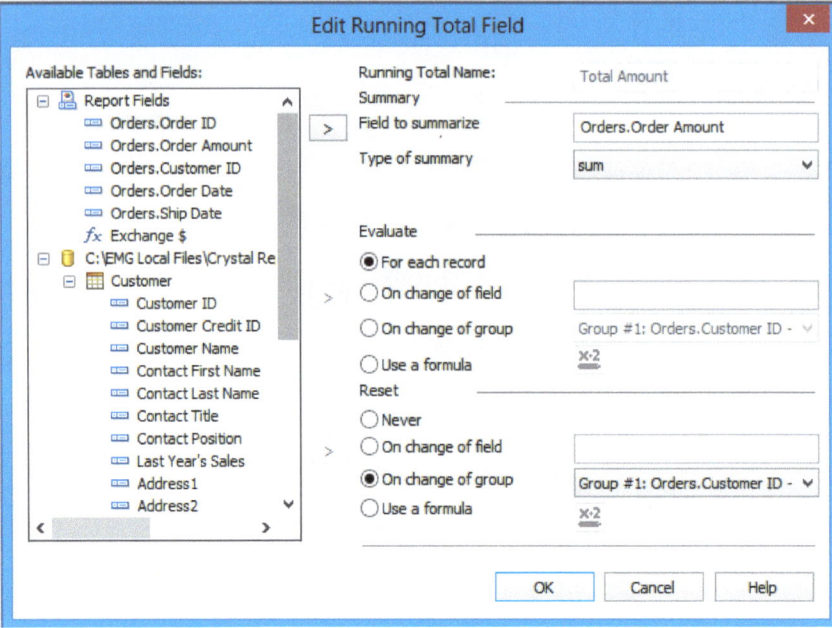

Type of Summary

Introduction Use the pull-down menu to display the Type of Summary for the Running Total field.

Options

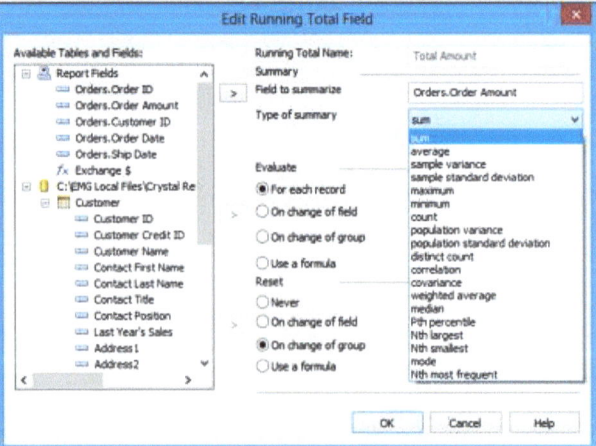

Evaluate Parameter

Introduction A Running Total field defaults at evaluating every record. In the case of a Type of Summary = SUM, the field of every record will be added.

Options
- For each record – Evaluates every record.
- On change of Field – Select a sorted field. The record is evaluated when the sorted record value changes
- On change of group – Select a Group. The record is evaluated when the Group value changes.
- Use a formula – Click on the [X-2] icon and enter a formula to determine the record to evaluate.

Reset Parameter

Introduction Reset parameter determines when the Running Total value is reset to zero. The default value is Never.

Options
- Never – Does not reset to zero
- On change of Field – Select a sorted field. The record is set to zero when the sorted record value changes
- On change of group – Select a Group. The record is set to zero when the Group value changes.
- Use a formula – Click on the [X-2] icon and enter a formula to determine when to reset the value to zero

Tips

Field Explorer Doesn't Launch

Issue   Field Explorer does not launch or display after selecting the Field Explorer icon or selecting View \ Field Explorer

Corrective Action
1. Go to **View**
2. Select **Toolbars**
3. Check the box next to "Reset all toolbars and explorers on the next restart."
4. Select **OK**

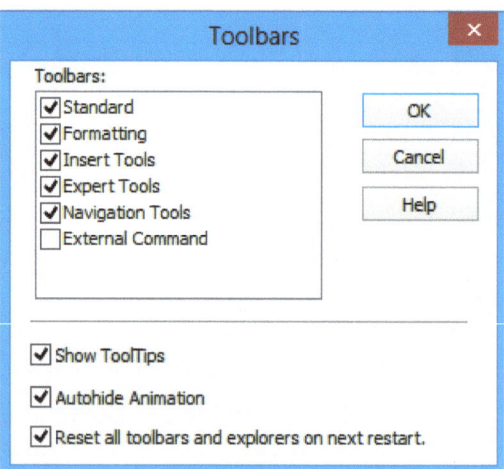

5. **Exit** Crystal Reports
6. Launch Crystal Reports
7. Open a report
8. Launch Field Explorer

Crystal Reports Crashes when Opening a Report File

Issue An error message appears as soon as you open a report file.

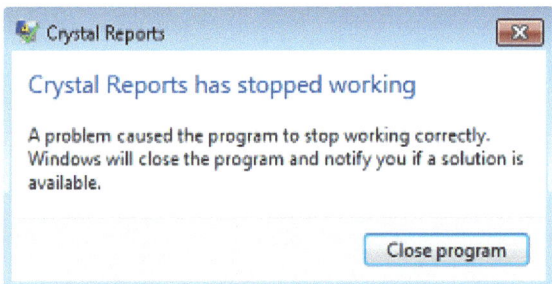

Corrective Action
1. Open the report file on an older version of Crystal Reports© such as Crystal Reports© XI.
2. Refresh the data
3. Save the file
4. Open report file in Crystal Reports© 2011

Intermediate Skills and Tips

Crystal Viewers

Report developers use Crystal Reports® 2011 to create report files. The report files can be executed routinely using a crystal viewer to pull updated data based on programmed data filters and user-defined parameters.

Crystal viewers are provided by SAP Data Objects or by third-party developers such as SaberLogic®, the makers of Logicity® crystal viewer. Use a web browser and search for "Crystal Reports 2011 Viewers" to see a list of available Crystal Viewers.

Select crystal viewers with the following features:
- Fully supports Crystal Reports® 2011 and older
- Opens report files directly
- Enable users to enter report parameters and refresh the data
- Export reports to Excel, PDF and other formats
- Free with unlimited use

Crystal viewers with advanced features, such as Logicity® Professional, are also available for sale. These advanced features include scheduling utilities to run reports, locking down screen controls, password protecting reports and encryption of report files.

Crystal Viewer

Shown below is an example comparison of features between a free-version crystal viewer and the paid-version of Logicity® by SaberLogic®.

Feature Comparison

How do the features of the free version of Logicity compare to the features of the Professional version?

Feature	Logicity (free)	Logicity Professional
Supports Crystal Reports v8.5, v9, v10, XI, 2008 & 2011	✓	✓
View Crystal Reports	✓	✓
Open Crystal Reports Files Directly	✓	✓
Refresh Crystal Reports Data	✓	✓
E-mail Crystal Reports	✓	✓
Save Crystal Reports	✓	✓
Export Reports to Word, Excel, and Other Formats	✓	✓
Centralized Report Scheduling	✓	✓
Logicity Solution Builder	✓	✓
Bar Code Fonts Included	✓	✓
Set Database User and Password per Report	✓	✓
Support for Dynamic/Cascading Parameters	✓	✓
Report Instances	✓	✓
Lock-down Screen Controls		✓
Encrypt Logicity Solution Files		✓
Password Protect Crystal Reports		✓
User Logging		✓
Socket Listening Mode		✓
Workspace Mode		✓
Open Non-Crystal Report Files		✓
Runtime Variables		✓
Command-Line Variable Replacements		✓
Encryption of Crystal Report Files		✓
Installation Support		Within first 30 days

Source: www.Logicitysuite.com

Beginner's Guide to Crystal Reports 2011

Installing and Using Logicity

1. Download and install Logicity® by SaberLogic®

    Note: Once installed, all Crystal Reports© files (*.RPT) will execute using Logicity® crystal viewer.

2. Double-click on the report file to launch the report using Logicity® crystal viewer

3. Enter User Parameters, if required

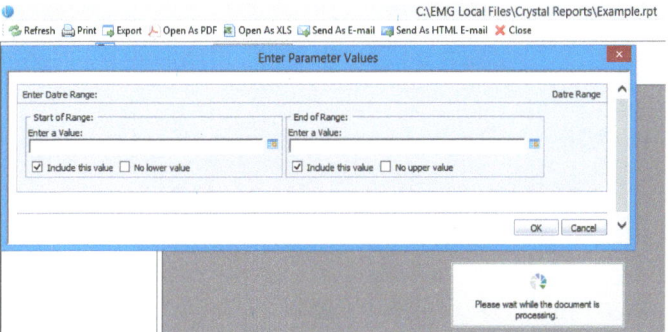

4. Use the report as designed

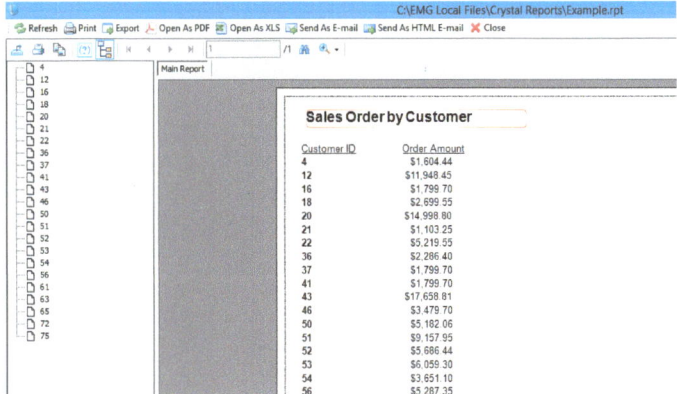

Logicity® Crystal Viewer Screen Functions

Refresh	Refresh the report data and if available, prompt for user parameters
Print	Send the report to a printer
Export	Save the report in a user-defined file type such as Excel, PDF, HTML or a Word file
Open to PDF	Display the report as a PDF file
Open as XLS	Display the report as a Microsoft© Excel file
Send as E-mail	Save the report in a user-defined file type such as Excel, PDF, HTML or a Word file, launch the default email utility, and attach the file to a new email.
Send As HTML E-mail	Save the report as an HTML file, launch the default email utility, and attach the file to a new email.
Close	Close the report file and Logicity© crystal viewer

Learning Resources

There are numerous learning resources available to expand the skills at using Crystal Reports. With the basic skills the reader can progress at using the free user manual available from SAP, use the Help utility within Crystal Reports© or search for Help topics using a web browser.

SAP Crystal Reports® 2011 User's Guide

1. Using a web browser, type "SAP Crystal Reports 2011 User's Guide"

2. Download the PDF file from help.SAP.com

Application Help Utility

1. Press F1 for Help utility

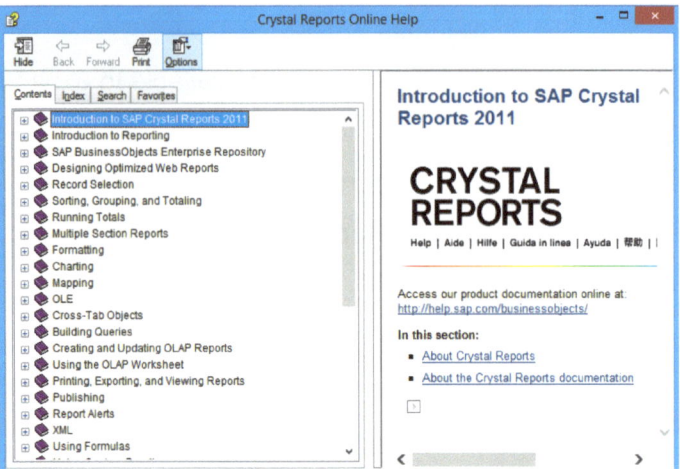

2. Select the Search tab to enter a specific topic

3. Select on the drop down menu or enter the topic to search

4. Press enter to list the topics

5. Double-click on the topic to display the Help details.

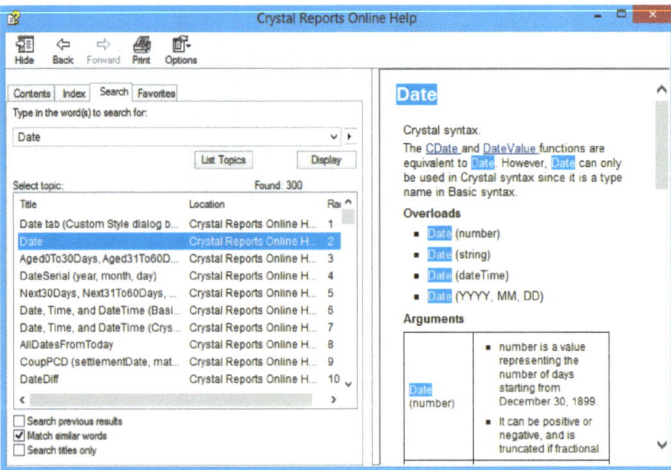

Web Community Help

1. Open a web browser

2. Type "Crystal Reports 2011 <help topic>" such as "Crystal Reports 2011 Running Totals"

3. Carefully select links and review Help notes

Index

A

Access/Excel · 18
accounting systems · 11
Adding a Graphic File · 35
Adding Text Fields · 86

C

Chart Expert · 69, 71, 72, 74
Chart Type · 74
Create New Connection · 17
Cross-Tab · 75, 77, 78, 79

D

Data Source · 3, 4, 20, 64
data table · 13, 15, 63
Database · 13, 14, 19, 24
DatePart · 88
Delimited Field · 89
Design · 35
Details · 23, 25, 31, 54, 55
Direct Access · 13
Drill-Down · 55, 56

E

ERP · 11, 12

F

Field · 13, 24, 27, 41, 43, 45, 47, 49, 50, 54
Field Format · 84
Filters · 37
Font Color · 84
Formatting · 27

G

Group · ii, 23, 28, 29, 48, 49
Group Footer · 23, 49
Group Header · 23

K

Key field · 13

L

Left · 87
Legend Box · 69, 71, 72
Linking Fields · 65
Logicity© · ii, 95, 96, 97, 98

M

Math Functions · 47
MRP · 11
Multiple Data Tables · 63, 67, 75, 81, 95, 99

N

New Connection · 18
New Data Connection · 17

O

obdcad32 · 4
ODBC connection · 3

P

Page Footer · 22, 68
Page Header · 22
Parameters · 37, 41
Preview · 25, 29, 30, 32, 34, 36, 40, 44, 49, 54, 56

Q

query files · 15

R

Record · 13, 31, 38, 43
Refresh Data · 40
Report Filter · 37
Report Footer · 22, 67, 69
Report Parameter · 37, 43
Right · 9, 10, 27, 41, 45, 47, 50, 55, 59, 60, 69, 71, 72, 74, 87
Running Total Field · 90
Running Totals Fields · 47

S

Select Expert · 38, 43
Split (x,y) [n] · 89
Standard Report · 17, 63
Summary Report · 55
Summary Reports · 55
System DNS · 3, 4
SysWOW64 · 3

T

Table · ii, 13, 21
Tables and Views · 20
Text Object · 33
ToText · 87

V

Value Field · 82
Value Options · 82
View · 13, 15, 46

W

Windows© 7 · 9
Windows© 8 · 10

X

Xtreme.mdb · 13

www.ingramcontent.com/pod-product-compliance
Lightning Source LLC
Chambersburg PA
CBHW040808200526
45159CB00022B/61